D1478352

MEDIEVAL GERMAN LYRIC VERSE

UNIVERSITY OF NORTH CAROLINA
STUDIES IN THE GERMANIC LANGUAGES
AND LITERATURES

Publication Committee

FREDERIC E. COENEN, EDITOR

WERNER P. FRIEDERICH   GEORGE S. LANE
JOHN G. KUNSTMANN   HERBERT W. REICHERT

32. Robert W. Linker. MUSIC OF THE MINNESINGERS AND EARLY MEISTERSINGERS. 1962. Out of print.
33. Christian Reuter. SCHELMUFFSKY. Translated into English by Wayne Wonderley. 1962. Out of print.
34. Werner A. Mueller. THE NIBELUNGENLIED TODAY. 1962. Out of print.
35. Frank C. Richardson. KLEIST IN FRANCE. 1962. Pp. xii, 211. Paper $ 5.00.
36. KÖNIG ROTHER. Translated into English Verse by Robert Lichtenstein. With an Introduction. 1962. Pp. xviii, 128. Paper $ 4.00.
37. John T. Krumpelmann. THE MAIDEN OF ORLEANS. A RomanticTragedy in Five Acts by Friedrich Schiller. Translated into English in the Verse Forms of the Original German. 2nd, Revised Edition. 1962. Out of print.
38. Rudolf Hagelstange. BALLAD OF THE BURIED LIFE. Translated into English by Herman Salinger. With an Introduction by Charles W. Hoffmann. 1962. Pp. xxii, 106. Paper $ 3.50.
39. Frederick R. Love. YOUNG NIETZSCHE AND THE WAGNERIAN EXPERIENCE. 1963. Out of print.
40. William H. McClain. BETWEEN REAL AND IDEAL. The Course of Otto Ludwig's Development as a Narrative Writer. 1963. Pp. x, 109. Paper $ 3.00.
41. Murray A. and Marian L. Cowie, Editors. THE WORKS OF PETER SCHOTT, 1460-1490. Volume I - Introduction and Text. 1963. Pp. xxxi, 359. Paper $ 7.50.
42. Herbert W. Reichert and Herman Salinger, Editors. STUDIES IN ARTHUR SCHNITZLER. Centennial commemorative volume. Introduction and 8 Essays. 1963. Out of print.
43. Clifford A. Bernd. THEODOR STORM'S CRAFT OF FICTION. The Torment of a Narrator. 1963. (See volume 55 below.)
44. J. W. Thomas. GERMAN VERSE FROM THE 12TH TO THE 20TH CENTURY IN ENGLISH TRANSLATION. 1963. Out of print.
45. Phillip H. Rhein. THE URGE TO LIVE. A Comparative Study of Franz Kafka's *Der Prozess* and Albert Camus' *L'Etranger*. 1964. *2nd* printing 1966. Pp. xii, 124. Cloth $ 5.00.
46. Edwin H. Zeydel. ECBASIS CUIUSDAM CAPTIVI. ESCAPE OF A CERTAIN CAPTIVE. An Eleventh-Century Latin Beast Epic. Introduction, Text, Translation, Commentary, and an Appendix. 1964. Out of print.
47. E. Allen McCormick. THEODOR STORM'S NOVELLEN. Essays on Literary Technique. 1964. Out of print.
48. C. N. Stavrou. WHITMAN AND NIETZSCHE. A Comparative Study of Their Thought. 1964. Pp. xiv, 233. Cloth $ 6.50
49. Herman J. Weigand. THE MAGIC MOUNTAIN. A Study of Thomas Mann's Novel *Der Zauberberg*. 1964. Pp. xii, 184. Cloth $ 6.00.
50. Randolph J. Klawiter. STEFAN ZWEIG. A BIBLIOGRAPHY. 1965. Pp. xxxviii, 191. Cloth $ 6.50.
51. John T. Krumpelmann. SOUTHERN SCHOLARS IN GOETHE'S GERMANY. 1965. Pp. xii, 200. Cloth $ 6.00.
52. Mariana Scott. THE HELIAND. Translated into English from the Old Saxon. 1966. Pp. x, 206. Cloth $ 6.00.
53. A. E. Zucker. GENERAL DE KALB, LAFAYETTE'S MENTOR. Illustrated. 1966. Pp. x, 252. Cloth $ 7.00.
54. R. M. Longyear. SCHILLER AND MUSIC. 1966. Pp. x, 202. Cloth $ 6.00.
55. Clifford A. Bernd. THEODOR STORM'S CRAFT OF FICTION. The Torment of a Narrator. Second, Augmented Edition. 1966. Pp. 160. Cloth $ 5.00.
56. Richard H. Allen. AN ANNOTATED ARTHUR SCHNITZLER BIBLIOGRAPHY. 1966. Pp. xiv, 151. Cloth $ 5.50.
57. Edwin H. Zeydel, Percy Matenko, Bertha M. Masche, Editors. LETTERS TO AND FROM LUDWIG TIECK AND HIS CIRCLE. 1967. Pp. xx, 395. Cloth $ 10.00.
58. STUDIES IN HISTORICAL LINGUISTICS. FESTCHRIFT for George S. Lane. Eighteen Essays 1967. Pp. xx 241. Cloth $ 7.50.
59. Wesley Thomas and Barbara G. Seagrave. THE SONGS OF THE MINNESINGER, PRINCE WIZLAW OF RÜGEN. Illustrated. 1967. Pp. x, 157. Cloth $ 5.50.
60. J. W. Thomas. MEDIEVAL GERMAN LYRICVERSE. In English Translation. 1968. Pp. x, 252. Cloth $ 7.50

For other volumes in this series see page 252.

Volumes out of print may be ordered from: AMS PRESS, Inc., 56 East 13th Street, New York, N.Y. 10003

Foreign Sales through:
Librairie E. Droz
11 Rue Massot
Geneva, Switzerland

NUMBER SIXTY

UNIVERSITY
OF NORTH CAROLINA
STUDIES IN
THE GERMANIC LANGUAGES
AND LITERATURES

Medieval German Lyric Verse

In English translation

J. W. THOMAS

CHAPEL HILL
THE UNIVERSITY OF NORTH CAROLINA PRESS
1968

Printed in the Netherlands by Royal VanGorcum Ltd., Assen

ACKNOWLEDGMENTS

The author would like to express his gratitude to Karen Doyle for her help in proof-reading the manuscript of this book, to Prof. Barbara Jarvis for contributing three translations to it (the second, third, and fourth by Wolfram) and for offering valuable criticism with respect to the other translations, and to Dean Adkisson and the Graduate Council of the University of Arkansas for a generous research grant. He is also indebted to the University of Illinois Press for permission to use material which appeared in *The Songs Of The Minnesingers*, by Barbara Seagrave and J. W. Thomas, and to the University of North Carolina Press for permission to use material from *German Verse From The 12th To The 20th Century In English Translation*, by J. W. Thomas, and from *The Songs Of The Minnesinger, Prince Wizlaw Of Rügen*, by J. W. Thomas and Barbara Seagrave.

CONTENTS

I

THE SONGS OF THE MONASTERIES

At the beginning of the twelfth century the written language in the German-speaking lands was Latin, and the only scribes were those who knew that language: the monks, priests, and nuns. Such literature, epic or lyric, as was produced in German was preserved for a while in an oral tradition, but then, except in a very few cases, it disappeared. A fragment of an early ninth century heroic poem, some heathen charms, a late ninth century eulogy of a Westfranconian king, several greater and lesser theological works: sermons, commentaries, and free translations of biblical writings—this is almost the total extent of German literature before the twelfth century which has been preserved.

Until the twelfth century the only centers of learning in Germany and the only links with the classical culture of the past were the monasteries and convents. Although throughout most of their previous existence these had been content to be strongholds of the faith and repositories of old manuscripts, in certain of them can be detected by the eleventh century a rather general interest in the literature of ancient Rome, particularly in the writings of Ovid, Plautus, Terence, and Vergil. This interest stimulated a much larger number of talented monks and nuns, not only in Germany, but throughout Western Europe, to produce literary works of their own, at first in Latin, but later in the vernaculars: French, German, and Provençal. Perhaps at least indirectly connected with the interest in classical literature and its exaltation of Venus was the development of a phenomenon which was to contribute to the courtly love song, that is, the cult of the Virgin. This produced a large body of literature, the Marian songs, and later influenced a great deal of erotic verse.

At about the same time that the monasteries were beginning to create many works of at least some literary value, events outside of the monasteries were taking place which strongly affected the cultural situation in the German–speaking lands. A new social class, the minor nobility usually referred to as the knights, had come into being and had become sufficiently numerous and prosperous to support a considerable amount of entertainment, and preferred it in their own language, German. Thus appeared the prerequisite for a secular literature, a secularly-minded audience. Many of these knights could write and others who could not were able to employ clerics to record the melodies and lyrics of such songs as they might compose. So it was that German lyrics no longer had to depend entirely on oral tradition for their preservation.

The knights, of course, were not limited exclusively to their own compositions for entertainment any more than was the general populace, for among the large number of professional entertainers—dancers, pantomimists, jugglers, and acrobats who moved from town to town much as do the county fair people of today—there were also poets, composers, and musicians, who were at once the creators, preservers, and disseminators of folk literature and music, and it was due to their efforts that the little which Germany still has of its pre-Christian literature has been saved. In the repertoires of the *Spielleute* (singular, *Spielmann*), as these wandering singers were called, were long narrative poems about ancient Germanic heroes, ballads concerning contemporary as well as past events, and songs for almost every occasion. The latter were short and simple in form and employed end-rhyme instead of the regular alliteration of older Germanic poetry. Unfortunately very little verse by these anonymous artists has been preserved and we know their song mainly as it is reflected in the compositions of minnesingers of the twelfth and thirteenth centuries and in the folksongs of later centuries.

The *Spielleute* provided entertainment for peasant as well as knight, but another class of performers, the goliards, had a clientele which was limited largely to the well-educated. The goliards consisted of defrocked priests, honest monks who were supporting themselves on their travels, and unemployed ex-students of the monastic schools. They composed and sang religious and secular songs, usually in Latin, sometimes in the vernacular, and occasionally in a surprising mixture of the two. The ranks of the itinerant clerics were swelled particularly by the success of the reform movement which, beginning at the Monastery of Cluny in the tenth century, gradually spread throughout Christendom. The strict rules of behavior which the movement caused to be enforced on the priests and in the monasteries induced many a pleasure-loving divine out into a world which was more than willing to support an artist who could compose and sing a good song, whether religious, didactic, or bawdy.

It was probably the Cluny reform movement that provided the initial impetus for the Middle High German literary awakening. For the movement, which at first was concerned solely with a purification of the clergy itself and a reform of church institutions, soon acquired an evangelistic zeal which aimed at the regeneration of all classes of society. Since the laymen knew no Latin, religious songs began to be composed and written down in German. The form in which these works appeared was doubtless influenced by that of the popular songs of the day because the audience for which both types of songs were composed was the same. At any rate, there exist similarities between popular secular songs and the lyrical products of the clergy from the twelfth century to at least the sixteenth century. The form is simple, of course, usually with short stanzas and either couplet or alternating rhyme. The rhyme is often impure, particularly with regard to consonants. This simplicity presents a marked contrast with the sophisticated virtuosity of the courtly song which developed toward the end of the twelfth century and reached its greatest complexity in the productions of the master-singers of the fifteenth and sixteenth centuries.

The earliest extant German lyric to be produced by the evangelistic activity of the monasteries is the 'Marian Song of Melk,' which was composed in Austria at the very beginning of the twelfth century, probably for choral singing. Mary is praised as

the mother of God, the precursor of the Savior, and the inter-
cessor for mankind. Much of the symbolism with which she is
described had already become standard usage in previous Latin
works. Although the language dates the work as a very early
one, the music which appears with it in the manuscript (of the
fifteenth century) is that of a fourteenth century French ballad.

THE MARIAN SONG OF MELK

(Jû in erde)

In the sod
did Aaron place his rod.
It bore almonds,
nuts so precious.
To bear this sweetness you began
without the aid of any man,
Sancta Maria.

On a bushy pyre
Moses saw a fire.
It did not burn the wood,
although above there stood
a tall and mighty flame,
your pureness to proclaim,
Sancta Maria.

Gideon, leader of Israel,
spread a lamb-skin. It befell
that the wool by heaven's dew
was dampened through and through.
Thus the power came to be
that gave to you fertility,
Sancta Maria.

Starfish, morning red,
field unplowed and dead,
a flower blossoms there,

4

it gleams so bright and fair
and all around adorns
as a lily mid the thorns,
Sancta Maria.

A mighty fishing line was made
and you were born from strand and braid
and shared the task it undertook.
God's power was the fishing hook
which held death fast until it died.
Through you, too, death was set aside,
Sancta Maria.

Isaiah, long ago,
knew you would come, and so
he said, from Jesse's stem
a branch would grow, and then
a blossom bloom therefrom:
he spoke of you and your Son,
Sancta Maria.

United at His birth
was heaven with the earth,
when ass and cattle mild
knew the holy Child,
your lap then, Blessed Dam,
was cradle for a lamb,
Sancta Maria.

The Child of God you bore
who saved us evermore,
whose holy blood was shed
to rescue us from death.
For this shall He be praised,
our hopes through Him you raised,
Sancta Maria.

You are a gate which heard
and opened to God's word,
you dripping honeycomb,
you precious spice unknown,
you're filled with peace and love
just like the turtledove,
Sancta Maria.

Sealed-off fountain,
locked-up garden,
in which flows balsam,
that smells like cinnamon,
you are like the cedar tree
which is always vermin-free,
Sancta Maria.

Cedrus in Libano,
rosa in Jericho,
you most precious myrrh
whose fragance spreads afar,
above the angels, over all,
you atone for Eva's fall,
Sancta Maria.

Eva brought a double death
and one of them is ruling yet.
A second Eva came
and brought us life again.
The devil said our days were few,
Gabriel told the word of God to you,
Sancta Maria.

A child was born to you, a maid;
your radiance will never fade;
you are like the sun,
from Nazareth it comes,
Jerusalem gloria,
Israel laetitia,
Sancta Maria.

You are heaven's queen,
the gate we enter in,
chosen to be God's house,
sacrarium sancti spiritus,
aid us with your power
in our dying hour,
Sancta Maria.

The second extant lyrical production of Middle High German literature is also a Marian song. It was composed about the middle of the century at the Arnstein Monastery in West Central Germany. The monastery was founded in 1139 when Ludwig III, the last Count of Arnstein, gave his castle and property to establish the institution, and it has been suggested that his pious wife, Guda, who, like her husband, became an inmate of the monastery, was the authoress of the song.

Unlike the preceding work it is not a hymn and was perhaps intended to be read rather than sung although strong influences of the Latin sequence can be seen. The 'Arnstein Marian Song' is a rather long work of about 325 lines, some of which have been destroyed by erasures in the manuscript. The content, in so far as it has been preserved, can be divided into the following parts: one, an appeal to the Virgin with a listing of the various symbols of the virgin birth; two, a hymn of praise in honor of the queen of heaven; three, a prayer to Mary for freedom from sin and for help in life, death, and resurrection; four, an appeal to Christ; five, a prayer to Mary as an intermediary to her Son; six, a recommendation of others; seven, a concluding hymn to Mary as queen of heaven. Once more, much of the language and symbols employed are those previously appearing in Latin sequences and other liturgical works. However, the work itself is not merely derivative. It reveals a sensitivity and delicacy of feeling and an awe of the miracle of the immaculate conception expressed in verse which has not been excelled by subsequent Marian lyrics.

(Daz himel und erden solde erfrouwen)

That heaven be glad and earth might cease to mourn
the child who came to still our grief was born.
He came to you and caused no single moan,
and as befits the Son of God alone.

Each day the sun sends forth a stream of light
and yet it never fades or grows less bright;
you are no less a virgin, Holy One,
because, without man's aid, you bore a son.

When you bore the child
you were undefiled,
pure, as was God's plan,
untouched by any man.
Who thinks that such a thing cannot be true
should look upon the glass, that's so like you.
The beams of sunlight penetrate the glass
and gleam and grow more radiant as they pass,
through the glass into the house they flow
and drive away the darkness as they go.
You are the shining glass through which there came
the light which saved the world from night and shame.
From you God's light shone into every land,
since we received our Savior at your hand,
who shines for you and Christianity,
and from its unbelief has set it free.
God's light found you and left behind no stain,
just as the sun does with the windowpane.

A third Marian song is exceptional in that its form reflects the
courtly rather than the popular tradition. The rhyme scheme
which it uses, *a a a a*, was most common at the time of the early
Provençal influence on the German minnesong, from about 1170
to about 1180, and indicates the approximate date of composition.

The song is a greeting to Mary which first appears in a fifteenth century manuscript. The place of origin has not been determined.

(Ave Maria, ain rôs ân alle dorn)

Ave Maria, rose without a thorn,
with evil deeds that I must mourn
have I betrayed Him thou hast born.
Maria, save me from His scorn.

Ave Maria, because thy Child is dead
who hung before thee and was red
with blood, help me receive the bread
of angels, when in death and dread.

Ave Maria, because His life's blood stole
from Him and wracked with pain thy soul,
just as the angry billows roll,
help me to reach a joyful goal.

Ave Maria, thou so true and kind,
O let an angel be assigned
to me when I leave the world behind.
Keep me from what the foe designed.

Composed during the second half of the twelfth century, the 'Sequence of Muri' is the earliest sequence in the German language which has been completely preserved. The work was written to fit the melody of the Latin sequence, *Ave praeclara maris stella*, but there is little resemblance between the two works in either content or mood. The German lyric presents few symbols and allegories and gives a simple presentation of the miracle of incarnation in sincere and pious language. Except in the early stanzas where the influence of the Latin original is the

9

strongest, the work has pure rhyme. It is also only in these first stanzas that it has a hymnal character.

It has been suggested that the author was a nun, but the only support for this assumption is that the song appears in two prayer books intended for nuns. The author was certainly an educated cleric, perhaps a Swiss, since both extant versions show Allemanic characteristics. The name is taken from the Monastery of Muri in Northern Switzerland where the chief manuscript was preserved for many years.

MARIAN SEQUENCE OF MURI

(Ave, vil liehtû maris stella)

Ave, radiant *maris stella,*
you light of Christendom, Maria
of every virgin a *lucerna.*

Rejoice then, God's own *cella,*
you closed and fastened *porta.*
When you bore the One
who formed both you and all the world,
how pure a vessel carried then God's Son.

Let me hear from you
the words so sweet and true,
Oh queen of heaven's host,
that I may praise your blessed Son
and praise the Father and the Holy Ghost.
A virgin you remain,
a mother without fault or stain,
through you is all that Eva lost restored,
who disobeyed her Lord.

Help me, Holy Maid,
console us who are sore afraid,
because God chose you, as did once foretell
the angel Gabriel.

On hearing what he said
your heart was filled with dread;
your virgin modesty
was shocked that, undefiled,
a maiden there might be
who still would bear a child.

You wonder as no other,
a maid and yet a mother!
He who conquered hell
within your body stayed;
you bore the infant well
and still remained a maid.

You are the gate to bliss. You heard
and then, made pregnant by the Word,
there came to you
a child through your ear,
the Lord of Christian, heathen, Jew,
whose grace and kindness never had an end.
You, Jewel of all maids,
were chosen well the child to tend.

Your majesty cannot be small,
for you, the purest maid of all,
bore Living Bread.
'Twas God Himself
who lifted to your breast his head
and took your breast in both his tiny hands.
Oh, my queen, what grace
has come to you through God's commands.

Oh give me your assistance when I pray,
that I shall trust in you, my lady, and with all
        my heart sincerely say,
what all can see
and none deny: that you're the mother of love
        and sympathy.

From what you've rendered may I profit too;
you took the holy Infant in your loving arms
    and held him close to you.
May you be blessed!
Help me because of Him; I know He'll grant you
    each request.

Your dearest Son can never turn aside His
    mother's prayer;
beg Him to grant me peace and save my heart
    from bitter care;

And, because he died, indeed,
for all mankind, ask Him to look
with kindness on my human need;

And, through the Holy Trinity,
be gracious to the sinful man
whom he has made in forming me.

When my soul departs, Oh lady, give your aid;
console my spirit then,
    for I believe that you are both a mother and a maid.

Not all of the verse which was written in the monasteries
was religious. Indeed, perhaps the earliest and, in the original,
one of the most charming love songs in the German language
was written in a cloister. The song 'Thou art Mine' appeared in
a Latin manuscript at the Tegernsee monastery in Southern
Germany. The work presents a correspondence in which a
monk in fervent and rhetorical language declares his love for a
nun. At the end the latter in a friendly manner directs his
ardor into the proper limits. The contrast between the sophis-
ticated Latin prose and the simple German song is quite striking.

THOU ART MINE

(Dû bist mîn)

Thou art mine,
I am thine,
that this is true thou shouldst divine.
Enclosed thou art
within my heart,
the key is lost, and by design:
thou must ever there recline.

Although we cannot be sure of its origin, it is quite probable
that the first crusade song originated in a monastery. The stanza
appears in a manuscript of the year 1422, but goes back to about
the middle of the twelfth century. The first line of the song is
repeated in Gottfried von Strassburg's epic poem, *Tristan*.

WE JOURNEY IN GOD'S HOLY NAME

(In gotes namen fara wir)

We journey in God's holy name,
His eternal grace we claim,
and we now implore His aid
and the holy grave's
where in human form He lay.
Kyrie eleison!

By the end of the twelfth century the fervor of the Cluny reform
was largely spent and a search for a harmonious union of worldly
joys and service to God can be seen not only in secular but also
in religious verse. However, the *vanitas mundi* theme of pre-
Renaissance Christianity frequently occurs throughout Middle
High German literature. Indeed, almost all of the poets who
have left a considerable amount of verse to posterity have com-
posed at least one song in which the singer rejects the world

13

and all its temporal pleasures. The following song was apparently composed by a knight who gave up secular life to become a monk. The date of composition was probably about the turn of the century.

OH MY YEARS, MY LOST AND WASTED YEARS

(Owê mîner gar virlornen jâre)

Oh my years, my lost and wasted years
that died before I left the world behind;
its love, so false, deceived my eyes and ears
and with its glitter turned my foolish mind.
Another love admonishes me thus:
it tells that Christ was sent to earth for us
and that his word will be our help and stay.
His love has brought me to a gown of gray.

Much of the verse that issued from the monasteries and cloisters was occasional in that it was composed to be sung at particular church festivals. The following song was first performed at a celebration of Pentecost, probably about the middle of the thirteenth century. It appears in a sermon of Berthold von Regensburg (died 1272) with the comment: 'It is a very useful song; you should sing it and call to God all the more gladly and with much reverence and with a sincere heart. It was a very good invention and a useful invention and it was a wise man who first invented this song.'

NOW ON THE HOLY GHOST WE CALL

(Nû biten wir den heiligen geist)

Now on the Holy Ghost we call
for true religion most of all,
that he keep us till the journey home
when in foreign lands we roam.
Kyrie eleison!

As one might expect, the Easter celebration inspired a large number of religious songs, in German as well as in Latin. One of the earliest in German is the one below, which has remained popular throughout the centuries and has often been expanded into longer songs. It first appears in a manuscript of the fifteenth century, but doubtless goes back at least to the thirteenth century.

CHRIST HAS ARISEN

(Christ ist erstanden)

Christ has arisen
free from every torment;
rejoice then all creation,
Christ is our consolation.
Kyrie eleison!

Halleluia, halleluia, halleluia;
rejoice then all creation,
Christ is our consolation.
Kyrie eleison!

An important source of religious verse and poetic prose in both German and Latin was mysticism. Although the mysticism of the German late medieval period is primarily associated with Master Eckhart, Heinrich Seuse, and Johannes Tauler, the most gifted writer among the mystics was none of these, but was Mechthild of Magdeburg. She was born about 1207 in Lower Saxony of well-to-do parents who probably belonged to the minor nobility. She was educated and was familiar with the courtly literature of the day, some of which is reflected in her religious writings. Her first mystic experience came at the age of twelve when she was so 'greeted by the Holy Spirit' that 'all the world's sweetness caused sorrow.' In about the year 1230 she went to Magdeburg in order to serve God and the sick as a lay nun. The strict asceticism that she practiced to restrain her own sensuality was rewarded by mystic visions and conversations which she wrote down from 1250 to 1265 and gave to her spiritual counsellor, Heinrich von Halle, who collected them into the work, *The Flowing Light of Divinity*, which was translated into High German about 1340. Since the original Low German version has been lost, we know the work only in its High German form and in a Latin translation of the latter. Around the year 1270 Mechthild entered the Cloister of Helfta, in Mansfeld, where she remained until her death some twelve years later. During this time she was the center of a productive literary group made up of young nuns with mystic leanings.

Mechthild was the first writer of German literature to write of the revelation of the heart of Jesus to herself. In her visions she saw the Trinity, the person of Christ in human form, the Virgin Mary, as well as angels and devils. The visions and conversations gave her courage to attack evils of the times, wisdom with which to enlighten her fellow clerics, and instruction concerning the intentions of divine providence. They lit in her a fire of mystic love for God which is expressed in a passionate language not unlike that of the courtly minnesong. One can even trace in them the influence of the courtly village songs of Neidhart. Like that of much mystic writing Mechthild's rhymed verse and rhythmical prose contains considerable sexual imagery. The soul is the loving queen and God holds it as His bride in the most intimate of embraces on the bed of love. Her writings reveal a thorough knowledge of the theological teachings and concepts of the day, expressed in professional terminology. She expounds on Biblical topics, on dogma, on asceticism, on the art of serious prayer. But her formal exposition is repeatedly interrupted by imaginative imagery and her prose frequently passes over into rhymed verse.

Mechthild's work did not greatly influence posterity, the rarity of the manuscripts is evidence of that; however, she was never completely forgotten. It has been argued, though not convincingly, that Dante was inspired by Mechthild's visions of the after-life and that he used her as a model for his Matelda.

(Swenne ich schine so muost du lühten)

When I glow, then Thou must flash,
when I flow, must wildly dash,
when Thou sighest, Thou drawest my godly heart into Thee.
I shall take Thee into my arms whenever Thou weepest for me.
When Thou lovest, then shalt Thou and I be one,
and when we two have become but one, then we may never
be parted anew,
but a blissful waiting shall dwell between us two.
Lord, I await the time with hunger and with thirst,
with hastening and lust,
till the radiant hour
when Thy godly lips with power
give to us the chosen word
which by none has e'er been heard,
but the souls alone
who have left their earthly home
and laid against thy lips their ear;
they understand why love's so dear.

(O du brennender berg, O du userwelte sunne)

Oh Thou wondrous sun, Oh Thou brightly burning mountain!
Oh Thou round, full moon, Oh Thou deep, unfathomed fountain!
Oh Thou unattainable height, Oh Thou clearness without
measure!
Oh wisdom without peer!
O compassion which no man has missed!
Oh strength that nothing can resist!
Oh crown of grace and honor,
the least of Thy creation still must praise Thee.

(Du solt minnen das niht)

Nothing love and be,
fly from entity,

thou shalt stand alone
and call no friend thine own.

Thou shalt never cease to strive
to free thyself from all material things.
Prisoners shalt thou unbind
and the free confine.
The sick shall have thy help,
but care not for thyself.
Thou shalt drink the water of pain
and light the fire of love with the wood of purity as well,
and truly in a wilderness shalt dwell.

(Swelch mensche wird ze einer stunt)

Whoever be the gallant swain
who suffers pangs of love in vain,
he never will be well again
till he from rosy lips obtain
a kiss from her who brought him pain.

(Were alle die welt mîn)

If the world belonged to me,
were naught but gold to see,
and if now and forever I might be
the noblest and most lovely empress in her majesty,
all this I'd soon surrender,
so gladly would
I see my saviour, Jesus Christ, the kind and good
in all his heavenly splendor.
Consider how they grieve who long must wait for him.

Although the writings of Mechthild were not greatly influential on her time, still they reflect the beginning of a significant cultural development which was to flower in the following century. The pre-Renaissance intellectual of the fourteenth century was painfully aware of the decline of scholasticism into specious argumentation over trivia and had lost the faith in the fundamental harmony between reason and revelation which had produced the dynamic ideas of Saint Thomas Aquinas and John Duns Scotus. In his search for a meaningful existence he turned from dogma and Aristotelian dialectics to a personal union on one basis or another with divinity or the spirit of divinity. It was the age of Eckhart, Seuse, and many lesser mystics, and the prevailing tone of the lyric verse of the monasteries and cloisters is one of longing for identification with Christ. Sometimes this longing is expressed in the imagery and symbolism of mysticism; sometimes, as in the following anonymous song, in more traditional language.

WEEP MY EYES AND WEEP MY HEART

(Wene herze, wenent ougen)

Weep my eyes and weep my heart,
weep with bloody tears of woe,
weep with others, weep apart,
weep, your tears have need to flow,
for I've lost a love whose worth
is so great I'd chosen it
over every love on earth.

Wandering as an orphaned waif,
seeking Him, my spirit's loss,
who from hell would keep me safe
through His death upon the cross,
I don't know where I should turn,
where to find my heart's desire,
for whose saving love I burn.

I was in a meadowland
happy in His loving care;
now I pass through barren sand,
since I lost Him unaware.
Sweetness, Thou, without alloy,
Jesus, Loved-one, let me find Thee
and with Thee regain my joy.

The last of the great German mystics of the fourteenth century, Johannes Tauler, was the son of a wealthy citizen of Strassburg. He was born about 1300 and at an early age entered a Dominican monastery where he began his study of theology. At some time during his youth he came into contact with Master Eckhart whose writings were greatly influential on all of Tauler's thought. Tauler soon became the most popular preacher in Strassburg and famous among the theologians of his day. As a result of the interdict quarrel between Emperor Ludwig of Bavaria and Pope John XXII, Tauler together with other clerics found sanctuary in Basel and remained there for several years. Later he returned to Strassburg, preached on occasion at various Rhineland cities, and journeyed as far as Brussels and Paris. Tauler's mysticism was of a more practical nature than that of Eckhart or Seuse and one can trace in it the beginnings of a Renaissance attitude. Although he speaks of the influx of divinity in the soul, he nowhere strives for the loss of personal identity. His influence can readily be seen on subsequent Christian theology, Protestant as well as Catholic.

The song below has been ascribed to Tauler. It was very popular and exists in numerous variant forms. The symbol of Mary as a ship is an old one which is derived from Proverbs 31, 14: 'She is like the merchants' ships; she bringeth her food from afar.' The word 'timeless' in stanza three is also symbolic in that it is the name of the yellow narcissus, an early flower whose appearance announces the approach of spring. The poem has a simple folksong quality and nothing of the ecstatic language or fanciful symbolism which is characteristic of the lyric verse of other mystics.

A SHIP COMES HEAVY LADEN

(Es kumpt ein schiff geladen)

A ship comes heavy laden
with cargo into view,
it brings the Son of the Father,
the Word forever true.

Upon the quiet waters
the little ship is seen,
it brings a gift so precious
from heaven's holy queen.

Oh Mary, fairest of roses,
where mercy and grace begin,
and timeless beauty reposes,
deliver us from sin.

The ship approaches in silence
and brings a treasure vast,
the sail is love eternal,
the Holy Ghost the mast.

21

2

SPIELMANN VERSE

Although the earliest extant Middle High German lyric verse was a product of the monasteries, it is obvious that there were *Spielmann* songs and a *Spielmann* tradition long before the clerics began to use German as a literary language. For the *Spielmann* was a direct descendent of the ancient Germanic scop, who, in turn, was the offspring of primitive ancestors who were composing and singing songs at the dawn of the human race. It is not surprising, however, that the early *Spielmann* verse was lost, since most of the *Spielleute* of the twelfth century and before could not write, and even such works as were written down were not likely to find their way to the relative safety of a library. Indeed, very few of the *Spielmann* songs were recorded before the middle of the fifteenth century. Then, and more particularly in the following century, they were collected as folksongs, some of which had been sung for hundreds of years. The authors of *Spielmann* lyrics are almost always unknown and verse can be so classified only on the basis of form and content — both aimed at popular rather than sophisticated audiences.

One of the most prevalent types of *Spielmann* verse was the riddle, a poetic genre which flourished throughout the medieval period and no doubt antedates it. The two following riddles first appear in a manuscript of the fifteenth century, but certainly go back at least to the twelfth century.

A WOOD WITHOUT A LEAF

(Welchs ist ein wald on laub)

Guess: A wood without a leaf,
         a land without a thief,
         a street that has no dust,
         a people all can trust,
         a house with no smoke above,
         a place that knows not love?

Answer: The wood is a pine forest, the land without
         a thief is heaven, the street is a well-travelled
         waterway, the people are Enoch and Elijah,
         the place that knows not love is hell.

THREE I SAW BOTH GREAT AND STRONG

(Ich sach drey starker, warn fast gross)

Guess: Three I saw both great and strong,
         they labored hard and labored long.
         The one spoke thus: 'I wish for night,'
         the other: 'Day for me, and light,'
         the third one: 'Whether night or day,
         I never rest along the way.'

Answer: The sun, the moon, and the wind.

The best known of the early riddle verse of the *Spielleute* is the
'Song of the Wanderer,' a poem appearing in a paper manuscript
of the fourteenth century which was used as a songbook by a
wandering singer. Some of the riddle-questions are found in
other versions in the folk literature of the present. Since the
Middle High German expression *varender man* means not merely
a wanderer, but more specifically a *Spielmann*, the song gives us
something of an insight into the life of these itinerant entertain-
ers. It was probably composed in the twelfth century.

(Willekome, varender man)

'Welcome here, Oh wanderer!
Where did you spend the night?
What sheltered you from cold and fright?
Tell me how and by what feat
did you get clothes and food to eat?'
'You have asked this of a man
who wants to answer truly everything, and can:
I was sheltered by the sky
and decked with many a rose was I,
I get as does a noble squire
the clothes and food which I desire.'
'Master Wanderer, I own
two–and–seventy lands to you are known—
what tree can bear without a bloom,
what bird gives milk to feed its young,
what bird is there which has no tongue,
what bird is there which has no craw?
I'll admit I never saw
a smarter youth if you can tell me all of that.'
'You have asked this of a man
who wants to answer truly everything, and can.
The juniper bears without a bloom,
The stork it is that has no tongue,
The bat gives milk to feed its young,
the cormorant's without a craw;
I'll tell you what I know and saw,
and if you ask me something more
I'll answer on your honor as before.'
'Master Wanderer, I own,
two–and–seventy lands to you are known—
what is whiter than the snow,
what is faster than the roe,
what is higher than the hill,
what is darker than the night?

If what you tell me is the truth
I'll admit I never saw a smarter youth.'
'You have asked this of a man
who wants to answer truthfully, and can.
The sun is whiter than the snow,
the wind is faster than the roe,
the tree is higher than the hill
and soot is blacker than the night;
still I shall say to you what's true and right:
if you ask me something more
I answer on your honor as before.'
'Master Wanderer, I own
two-and-seventy lands to you are known—
tell me why the Rhine's so deep,
or why the ladies are so sweet,
what makes the meadows all so green,
and knights so bold with haughty mien?
If what you tell me now is true
I'll know that you're a really clever youth.'
'You have asked this of a man
who wants to tell you, and he can.
Because of many springs the Rhine is deep,
because of courtly love are ladies sweet,
because of many roots are meadows green,
great wounds give knights a haughty mien;
and if you ask me something more
I'll answer on your honor as before.'
'Master Wanderer, I own
two-and-seventy lands to you are known—
why's the forest dark and gray,
the wolf much wiser than its prey,
the coat of arms so worn and dimmed;
why are good fellows often parted from their friends?
If what you tell me is the truth
I'll know that you must be a very clever youth.'
'You have asked this of a man
who knows, and gladly tells you all he can.
Because of age the forest is so gray,

the wolf learned wisdom from a cunning prey,
from many wars the coat of arms is dimmed,
and faithlessness will always part the best of friends.'
'Master Wanderer, I own
two-and-seventy lands to you are known—
What is green as clover, though
it is also white as snow?
What is black as any coal,
and what ambles like a foal?'
'I can quickly tell you that:
A magpie is as green as clover, though
it is also white as snow
and is just as black as coal
and it ambles like a foal,
and if you ask me something more
I'll answer on your honor as before.'

The first of the German ballads, 'The Kerenstein Ballad,' was
probably the composition of a *Spielmann* of the third quarter of
the twelfth century. Although it first appears in a fifteenth
century manuscript, the language, the long line, and the occasion-
al impure rhyme taken together betray a much earlier origin.
And, although the characters belong to the knightly class, the
tone of the ballad is popular rather than chivalric. In the ballad
the watchman who guards lovers and comments on their affairs,
a standard figure in the courtly dawn song, first comes into
German verse. It is he who speaks in the last stanza.

THE KERENSTEIN BALLAD

(Ich bin durch frawen willen   geritten in fremdeu land)

Because of a lady I journeyed   afar to a distant land,
I rode there as a herald   at a noble knight's command.
'He sends me, lovely lady,   with his regards to you.
You make him very happy: what would you like to have him
                                                                          do?'

'What message should I send him?'   was what the maiden said.
'But I would be so happy   to see the man, instead.
Look yonder at the linden   beneath the castle wall
and tell your lord to wait there   for me soon after evenfall.'

When the knightly noble   arrived at the linden tree,
he found beneath the linden   a maiden fair to see.
At once he took his mantle   and threw it on the grass
and there the two were lying   until the long, long night had
                                                            passed.

'You've gotten what you wanted,'   thus spoke the lovely
                                                            maid,
'and now it seems you'll leave me   alone, so I'm afraid,
and turn your back upon me   and quickly ride away.
Then I'll be like a little child   and weep for you to stay.'

'You wondrous, lovely lady,   I won't permit your eyes
to weep, for I shall shortly   return to take my prize;
look and see my charger   that's standing over there.
He'll bear you, loveliest of all,   from danger and despair.'

Then there came from the castle   a mighty blast of sound
and on the wall the watchman   sang: 'Gates are open now.
Who's suffered any losses   will come to know it soon.'
Then spoke the Lord of Kerenstein: 'My pretty daughter, Oh
                                                            is gone.'

'Now Christ in heaven knows this: I've only done what's
                                                            right
and if my charming maiden   has left us for a knight,
then that was what both wanted—   their love was deep and
                                                            strong.'
The watchman high above them   sang out a pretty morning
                                                            song.

In many ways the literature of the twelfth century is most similar
to that of the eighteenth century: in the emphasis on moderation,

good taste, sentiment, form, and especially on education. Not only in the monastic writings, but also in the courtly, goliard, and *Spielmann* lyric one finds considerable didacticism. Such instructive verse, the *Spruch*, consists usually of a single stanza and, like love verse, was sung. The following *Sprüche* from several twelfth century manuscripts give advice on a variety of personal matters as well as, in the case of the last poem, some bitter social criticism.

A FORD THAT'S DARK AND WIDE

(Tief furt truobe)

A ford that's dark and wide,
to sleep with others' wives,
who's careless here will know
his share of bitter woe.

THE BITTER WORLD IS HARD TO PLEASE

(Al die werlt mit grimme stet)

The bitter world is hard to please,
who loafs about and takes his ease
will find himself undone
and all his honor gone.

WHO GOES TO CHURCH CONTENT

(Der zi kilchen gat)

Who goes to church content
and there does not repent
is, on the judgment day,
struck down and cast away.
And who is there condemned
his pain shall never end.

(Ubermuot diu alte)

Old arrogance will ride
with violence at his side
while falseness holds his banner high
and greed goes forth to terrify
the orphans everywhere.
The land is fearful of the harm that it must bear.

One of the few *Spielleute* of the twelfth century whom we can
identify, if only by a pseudonym, is listed in several manuscripts
as Spervogel. According to tradition there were two singers
who used this name and tradition has some support in the fact
that two slightly different metrical patterns (*Töne*, singular, *Ton*)
are employed. We know nothing of the lives of either of the
Spervogels. They were doubtless wandering singers, probably
Bavarians, and composed approximately between 1260 and 1280.
The Spervogel texts are characterized by simplicity of form,
concise and often forceful language, and an imaginative use of
homely metaphors and symbols. They contain a great deal of
religious and moral wisdom, sometimes expressed in short
parables and animal fables. An early fourteenth century manu-
script contains the melody to which many of the Spervogel
lyrics were sung.

A WOLF WAS FEARFUL FOR HIS SOUL

(Ein wolf sine sünde floch)

A wolf was fearful for his soul,
he joined a cloister, donned a stole:
this life he much preferred.
They sent him out to guard the herd
and he forgot his creed.
He tore the sheep and swine
and swore the bishop's dog had done the deed.

(Weistu wie der igel sprach)

Listen to what the hedgehog said:
'It's nice to have a home and bed.'
Build you a house, my boy,
seek there for peace and joy.
The lords are miserly.
Who doesn't have a house and home
much happiness will never see.

WHEN A FRIEND WILL ALWAYS STAND BESIDE HIS FRIEND

(Swâ eyn vriunt dem andern vriunde bîgestat)

When a friend will always stand beside his friend
with loyal hand and heart whenever woes descend,
then is his willing hand an aid
to him whose friendship is repaid,
and when they each support the other,   then their strength
                                                        increases.
When friends will help each other   they have joy which never
                                                        ceases.

The *Spielleute* of medieval Germany are probably of less significance for their own productions than for the fragments and remnants of the literature of the heroic age which they preserved, although usually in a somewhat altered form. The most important of the few extant documents of German pagan literature is 'The Song of Hildebrand,' a work which is thought to have originated in the sixth century, although the earliest written version dates from about the year 800. Hildebrand was probably an historical figure, a close friend of the Gothic king, Theodoric the Great, better known in German literature as Dietrich of Bern (Verona). The theme of the song is the father-son conflict. The narrative breaks off just as the combat begins, but we know from other sources that the father is forced by his strong, primitive sense of honor to kill his own son. The original has the bold realism and stark tragedy characteristic of the songs of the Germanic scops. However, as the story continued to be passed down by generations of *Spielleute* into more gentle and sentimental times the hard lines disappeared and a mutual recognition makes the tragic ending unnecessary. Such is 'The Younger Song of Hildebrand,' of which we first hear in the thirteenth century, although the earliest extant manuscripts are of more recent origin. The popular nature of the song is indicated by occasional impure rhyme and metrical irregularities. A melody has been preserved.

THE YOUNGER SONG OF HILDEBRAND

('Ich wil zu land aussreiten,' sprach sich maister Hiltebrant)

'I'm going on a journey,'   thus spoke Sir Hildebrand,
who'll tell me of the passage   into Verona's land?
It's been so long I know not   the road to the frontiers,
for I've not seen Dame Uta   for two-and-thirty years.'
'Ride out in that direction,'   then said Duke Amelung,
'and you'll meet on the meadow   a warrior, brave and young;
you'll meet him on the border,   the young Sir Alebrand,
and if you were a dozen,   he'd charge you and your band.'
'Yes, should he try so proudly   to drive me from the field
he won't be very happy,   for I shall split his shield
and cut his breastplate open   with just a single blow;
his mother then will hear him   lament a year or so.'
But Dietrich of Verona   spoke up, 'It shall not be;
young Alebrand has always   been very dear to me.
Display a friendly manner,   because it is my will,
that he may let you enter.   I do not wish him ill.'
He rode from Rosengarden   to where Verona lay
and found himself in danger   from one who barred the way.
A bold and youthful warrior   approached with this demand:
'What do you seek, old fellow,   in this, my father's land?
You wear a suit of armor   a monarch's son would prize,
the metal gleams so brightly   it blinds my seeing eyes;

you should not journey hither,   but stay at home instead
and sit beside the fire.'   The old man laughed and said:
'Should I not journey hither,   but stay at home instead?
My life-long I've been sitting   behind a horse's head
to ride and fight in battles   until I pass away;
I tell you truly, youngster,   that's why my hair is gray.'
'I'll tear your beard, I tell you,   old man, right off your face
so that from cheek and jowls   the rose-red blood will race;
your shield and shining armor   I'll carry from the strife
and you will be my captive,   if you would save your life.'
'My armor and my buckler   are able friends and true
and they and Christ in heaven   will keep me safe from you.'
The warriors stopped their talking,   two keen-edged swords
                                        were drawn,
and that which both were seeking: a battle, soon was on.
The young man struck the other,   just how, I do not know,
so well and hard old Hildebrand   was startled by the blow,
full seven fathoms backwards   he staggered from the stroke;
'You learned that from a woman,   my boy,' the old man spoke.
'That I should learn from women   is shame I would not stand;
I've many knights and warriors   within my father's land,
the knights and counts are many   who stay at father's court,
and what I've not yet mastered,   I'll learn,' was his retort.
The older knight was stronger;   he seized him, threw him
                                        down
upon his back and held him   securely on the ground.
'Confess to me, young fellow,   for I shall be your priest,
if you're a wolf-cub, maybe   I'll change you from a beast.
Who rubs against old kettles   likes soot, you must agree,
and you'll get black, young fellow,   when you start rubbing
                                        me.
You'll give me your confession   right here on this green field;
I tell you, youthful warrior,   let nothing be concealed!'
'You speak of wolves, they wander   among the forest trees,
but I'm a noble warrior;   my fathers came from Greece.
My mother's Lady Uta,   a duchess without peer,
Old Hildebrand, the hero,   he is my father dear.'
'If Uta is your mother,   a duchess without peer,

I'm Hildebrand, the hero,   and am your father dear.'
He opened up his helmet   and kissed him, then he said,
'Praise be to God in heaven,   we're neither hurt nor dead!'
'Oh father, dearest father!   the wounds I gave you now,
Oh I would three times rather   have cut them in my brow.'
'Beloved son, be quiet,   I treasure every one,
since God has brought together, a father and his son.'

Of all of the lyrical compositions of the *Spielleute* the best known is 'The Ballad of Tannhäuser,' a work which was probably composed in the late thirteenth century although the earliest manuscripts are of the fifteenth century. This is the work which inspired Wagner's opera. The Venus Mountain is mentioned in Gottfried's *Tristan and Isolde* and the theme was doubtless very old even at that time. In essence it goes back to the Christianization of the Germans and the attacks of the Christian missionaries on their pagan mythology. Variant forms of the Venus Mountain theme appear throughout German folk literature; one such tale was borrowed by Irving for his 'Rip Van Winkle.' One can only guess as to how the minnesinger Tannhäuser happened to become connected with the legend. Perhaps it was a result of the sharp contrast between his light-hearted, satiric songs and those which bewail the poverty that resulted from his extravagant ways. In none of the undisputed Tannhäuser songs does there appear any concern about the welfare of his soul or sorrow for his sins. However, some of the verse which medieval collectors listed under his name has such content. It is generally believed that these latter songs were attributed to Tannhäuser as a result of the ballad. The pope mentioned in the ballad was Urban IV (1261-1264).

THE BALLAD OF TANNHÄUSER

(Nun will ich aber heben an)

I shall now begin to sing
Tannhäuser's song which tells

the strange adventures which he had
where Lady Venus dwells.

Tannhäuser was a knight who sought
adventure everywhere,
he entered Venus Mount to see
the lovely women there.

'Tannhäuser, I am fond of you;
hold that in memory,
and that you've sworn to me an oath
that you'd be true to me.'

'Dame Venus, that I did not do!
You know it's just a lie,
and if some other one said this,
God helping me, he'd die.'

'Tannhäuser, why must you lament?
Remain with me for life
and I shall give my friend to you
to be your loyal wife.'

'And if I took another wife
than her for whom I yearn,
then in the flaming fire of hell
eternally I'd burn.'

'You speak so much of flaming hell
but never felt its power:
just think about my ruby lips
which laugh at any hour.'

'I care not for your ruby lips;
they've brought me only woe.
Do honor now to womankind,
dear lady, let me go!'

'Tannhäuser, would you take your leave?
You shall not go away!
Remain with us, Oh noble knight,
and let your life be gay.'

'My life grows sadder all the time;
to stay is but to grieve.
Give me permission, lady fair,
that 1 may take my leave.'

'Tannhäuser, do not babble so,
what are you thinking of?
Let's go into my chamber now
and play the game of love.'

'For me your love is only pain;
I've opened up my eyes
and seen in you, my lady fair,
a devil in disguise.'

'Tannhäuser, what is this you say;
am I the one you scold?
If you remain in here you'll wish
you hadn't been so bold.'

'Dame Venus, that I shall not do;
I'll never stay in here.
Maria, mother, Holy Maid,
in my distress be near!'

'Tannhäuser, you may take your leave;
though you must lend your tongue
and sing my praises through the land,
but only to the young.'

He left the mountain then behind,
repentant and in grief.

'I'll go to Rome and trust the pope
to give my soul relief.

'I'll journey forth upon my way
(may God my life control)
to ask the pope who's called Urban
If he can save my soul.

'Ah, Pope, my comforter and lord,
my heart is filled with rue
because of all the wrong I've done
and now confess to you.

'With Venus I have spent a year,
a sin, as I know well.
I seek for absolution now
that I with God may dwell.'

The pope was leaning on a staff
and it was dry and dead.
'This shall have leaves e'er you receive
the grace of God,' he said.

'Had I a single year to live,
I'd spend it all to win
through any penance I could do
God's pardon for my sin.'

He went forth from the city's gate
in grief and sick at heart.
'Maria, mother, Holy Maid,
from you I now must part.'

He journeyed to the mountain then
to stay eternally.
'I'll go to see my lady sweet
where God would have me be.'

'Tannhäuser, welcome once again
you've been away so long.
I welcome you, my dearest lord
and lover, fair and strong.'

The third day when he took his staff
the pope saw leaves thereon.
He sent forth men to every land
where Tannhäuser might have gone.

But he was in the mountain there
with Venus as before,
and so the Pope Urban the Fourth
was lost for evermore.

3

GOLIARD SONGS

Most of the goliard songs which have been preserved appear in a single manuscript, the *Carmina burana*, which, although now in Munich, was formerly in the Abbey of Benediktbeuern; hence the name. The collection includes a wide variety of songs composed during the twelfth and thirteenth centuries, the majority in Latin, some in German. There are songs of a clerical or polemic tendency, drinking songs, nature songs, and love songs. As one scholar says, it is the lyrical verse of a happy, wandering, educated youth, which sang of wine, spring and dancing, antique gods, stupid peasants and avaricious priests, and whose high spirits often became bold sarcasms. Although many of the songs are full of piety and characterized by a delicate sensitivity, others are coarsely secular and frivolous, more heathen-antique than Christian. And, though some of the songs in the collection were composed after the development of the courtly song, they were not greatly influenced by the latter and resemble the *Spielmann* lyrics in spirit, if not always in form.

The first selection below is a dancing song which would have been sung while a group danced on the village green. It has a folksong rhythm and form, but one characteristic of the courtly song appears in it—the personification of love in the second stanza. 'Love' here takes the place of Venus of classical song.

(Ich wil trûren varen lân)

I shall cease to grieve and mourn.
To the blooming heath and thorn,
all my playmates, let us go!
There we'll see the flowers' glow.
I say to thee, I say to thee,
my lover, come with me.

Sweet and gentle Love of mine,
for me a wreath of blooms entwine!
This a stately man must wear,
one who serves a lady fair.
I say to thee, I say to thee,
my lover come with me.

One of the loveliest of the goliard songs is the following sensitive
and expressive stanza in which a peasant girl tells of her fear
that she has been forsaken and of her need for affection. The
second song describes a similar situation from the masculine
standpoint and contains a certain wry humor. Although there
are pretty, single girls all around, he has not been doing so well.

FLORET SILVA UNDIQUE

Floret silva undique,
how can he remain away?
Everywhere the woods are green,
yet my man has not been seen.
He's gone and thinks not of me;
alas, who's there to love me!

(Swaz hie gât umbe)

These walking here
are maids, it is clear,
but all of them plan
to spend this summer without a man.

The stanza below is the last of a three-stanza song, the first two
of which are entirely in Latin. They tell of a girl who is standing
in a red dress which rustles when one touches it; she stands like
a rosebud, her face beams and her red mouth blossoms. Here
we have the familiar association between the color red, the rose,
and love. The stanza given is humorous not only in its use of
mixed speech, but also in its ironical use of the terms *caritatem
magnam* and 'courtly love.' *Caritas* is spiritual love and 'courtly
love' is one which stresses longing without fulfillment, neither
of which is appropriate to the situation. The language of the
original would indicate that it was composed during the early
courtly period, for, although it speaks of courtly love, the poem
still uses assonance in place of pure rhyme.

STETIT PUELLA BY A TREE

(*Stetit puella* bî einem boume)

Stetit puella by a tree,
scripsit amorem on a leaf.
quickly then did Venus come,
caritatem magnam,
courtly love she offered her man.

One of the goliard lyrics which was directly influenced by the
courtly love song is 'Nightingale, Oh Sing a Ditty Fine.' Both
the 'fair and haughty queen' and the rhyme scheme are typical
of the chivalric, rather than the popular love song.

(Nahtegal, sing einen dôn mit sinne)

Nightingale, Oh sing a ditty fine
to this fair and haughty queen of mine!
tell her that my heart and spirit   ever burn and pine
for her self and for her love divine.

The following two stanzas apparently belong together as a single poem. The 'queen of England' is Eleanor of Poitou (1122-1204), an enthusiastic patron of the troubadors. The name is used humorously as a disguise for another and as a compliment to the real object of the singer's affections. The 'secret love' of the second stanza is one of the conceits of courtly love in that no one was supposed to know the object of the knight's sentiment. The praise of 'secret love' is apparently an extolling of the chivalric ideal of the knight's serving his lady-love with no hope of recompense.

WERE ALL THE WORLD MINE

(Waer diu werlt alliu mîn)

Were all the world mine
from the sea to the Rhine,
I'd give it away
if in my arms the lovely queen of England lay.

Secret love is beautified,
it can fill a man with pride.
One should seek it ever.
Who's unfaithful in this task deserves our praises
                                  never.

Although they form a rather small minority of the stanzas, it is chiefly for the bawdy lyrics that the *Carmina burana* is renowned. The seduced and forsaken maiden has been a popular theme for folksongs in all literatures from early times. However, in the verse of 'I Was a Child and Fair to See,' there is none of the sad sentimentality of the folksong. The account of the seducer's impatient passion and the impossibly naive deception of the girl are both intended to be amusing. There is some satire of courtly love in that the man pretends that he wishes the girl to come with him so that he can serenade her.

I WAS A CHILD AND FAIR TO SEE

(Ich was ein chint so wolgetan)

I was a child and fair to see,
virgo dum florebam,
and everyone commended me,
omnibus placebam.

Refrain: *Hoe et oe!*
maledicantur tilie
iuxta viam posite!

The fields I wandered unaware,
flores adunare,
a wicked stranger met me there,
ibi deflorare.

He took me by my snow-white hand,
sed non indecenter,
and led me o'er the meadowland,
valde fraudulenter.

He grasped me by my garment white,
valde indecenter,
and pulled at me with all his might,
multum violenter.

He spoke then: 'We must hurry on,
nemus est remotum.'

I wish that I had never gone,
planxi et hoc totum.

'There stands a linden, pretty maid,
non procul a via,
my harp is lying in its shade,
tympanum cum lyra.'

When the tree was overhead,
dixit: 'sedeamus,'
spurred by passion then he said:
'*ludum faciamus!*'

He seized me then without ado,
non absque timore.
'I'll make a woman now of you,
dulcis es cum ore!'

He pulled my clothing off in haste,
corpore detecta,
and straight into my castle raced,
cuspide erecta.

He took his quiver and his bow,
bene venabatur!
And this was he who tricked me so.
'*Ludus compleatur!*'

Among the more popular literary subjects of the medieval period
was the story of the snow child, which appears in several Latin
versions, a French version, and two German versions. The
earliest extant treatment is a Latin one contained in an eleventh
century manuscript. It is the best of the songs on this theme
and was sung to a particular melody which is indicated. The
translation which follows was made from the older German
version, which was composed in the thirteenth century by an
unknown Middle German poet and which is extant in a number

of manuscripts. The song is especially interesting to the medievalist in that the variant extant treatments clearly illustrate the changes which can occur in content and language as a poem is handed down through an oral tradition. The most important differences in the content of the story have to do with the husband's account of the disappearance of the boy; in some versions it is the hot southern sun that causes him to melt away. So it is in the Latin tale in the Cambridge Manuscript, from which all of the others seem to have descended. It is, of course, possible that this early Latin work was a translation or adaptation of a lost German song, from which the later German and French treatments came. However, the fact that the Cambridge Manuscript refers to goliards as the seducers of the woman make it probable that the work began as a goliard rather than as a *Spielmann* song. The same version identifies the merchant as a Swabian of the city of Constance.

THE SNOW CHILD

(Ez het ein koufman ein wîp)

A merchant had a wife
as dear to him as was his life.
She said his fondness was returned,
but still her heart had never learned
to love him too,
and it could not be true.
At last there came the day
he had to go away.
He left his house and wife as well
with many goods he hoped to sell
and sailed away upon the sea,
for thus a merchant's life must be.
He came into a foreign land
where wares as his were in demand.
So gainful was the trade
three years he stayed.
And when he journeyed home at last

the fourth year, too, was nearly past.
His wife then greeted him with joy,
but with her was a baby boy.
'Now tell me,' said he,
'whose child might this be?'
She spoke: 'My lust for you was so
as I was walking through the snow
I put some in my mouth to melt.
Then suddenly your love I felt
and later on the baby came.
I swear, the child deserves your name.'
'It well may be,' her husband smiled,
'that you are right; we'll raise the child.'
And so she never knew
he thought she was untrue
and all was just a lie
till more than ten years had gone by.
He taught the child on many walks
to hunt with dogs and use the hawks
in falconry and play at chess
and every sort of happiness;
he taught him manners and discipline,
to play the harp and violin,
the gamba and the lute
and many a gay pursuit.
   One day he ordered that his men
prepare his ship to sail again;
they loaded stores and made it trim.
He took the son-of-snow with him
and set forth on a stormy sea
with winds that drove them aimlessly.
He came upon a land most fair
and found a wealthy merchant there
who asked that he would tell
just what he had to sell.
The snow-son was offered, and was sold;
three hundred marks he brought, in gold,
and that's a lot, one must admit.

He won renown because of it;
he'd not been fooled in any way
when he had let the bastard stay.
What he'd endured would be repaid
with half of what he made.

　　Now he lingered there no more,
but journeyed toward his native shore.
His wife was waiting by the sea
and there received him lovingly.
But then she asked him, 'Where's the child?'
He spoke: 'The wind was wild,
though we did what we could,
it drove us anywhere it would.
The child was drenched and, I declare,
he changed to water then and there.
It should not have surprised me so,
because you told me he came from snow.
But, if it is true what I've heard said,
you need not mourn him as if he were dead.
No water ever flows so swift
that it does not in some way drift
back to the source within a year
from whence it came— that's what I hear.
Believe me, what I say is true,
it soon will flow again in you.

　　And thus he showed at once
that he was not a dunce.
Whatever man believes
his loving wife deceives,
just let him turn on her the ill,
and when she's smart, be smarter still—
in this he shows that he is wise,
for women have with wiles and lies
fooled more of men, without a doubt,
than you have ever heard about.

4

EARLY SINGERS OF THE NOBILITY

The secular culture which developed in Germany during the twelfth century and produced one of the nation's most significant literary periods was the result of many diverse factors, the most important of which were the First Crusade, which took place shortly before the century began, and the Second Crusade which was carried out some fifty years later. These crusades brought Germans into contact with the cultures of Byzantium and the Near East, cultures which stressed the enjoyment of life and had produced the means whereby man's desire for beauty, comfort, and pleasure might be satisfied. And the trade which resulted exposed Germany not only to the luxuries: the silks, spices, and perfumes, but also to some of the art and literature of the East. The crusades also brought Germany into closer economic and cultural relations with Italy, France, Provence, and even with the Moorish kingdom of Spain. The country for the first time came to know something of Mediterranean life.

The class which became acquainted with the cultures of the South and the Near East as a result of the crusades was that of the *Ministeriale*, usually referred to as the knights, who were the holders of small feudal grants. It was to them that the emperor Konrad II turned to build up his armies for the Second Crusade, and it was with them that his Hohenstaufen successors allied themselves in their struggle to increase the power of the empire at the expense of the individual German princes. The greater military and political importance which this alliance gave to the knights brought with it an increased class-consciousness which soon developed its own unique and highly idealistic code of ethics and morality—chivalry.

Chivalry was an all-embracing creed that determined the knight's varied activity and in which he was as carefully schooled as was the priest in his theology. Chivalric training in military skills and in a meticulous social etiquette began in boyhood and lasted until, in his early twenties, the page became a knight. But chivalry was more than a military and social code. Its chief goal was the achieving of a perfect balance between temporal and spiritual good, a harmonious union of the diverse elements of the knight's heritage: the Germanic virtues of loyalty and bravery, the humanity and compassion of Christianity, and the Greek and Oriental delight in beauty, grace, and form. A central element of chivalry was the idealization of woman and the cult of *minne*. Although medieval singers who used the term frequently disagreed as to its meaning, the general conception of *minne* is that of an erotic passion which is both physical and spiritual, but which reaches no fulfillment. Although it does not appear in the earliest songs of the knights, but entered later by way of Provence, the idea of *minne* received almost immediate acceptance among German nobility for it filled an aesthetic and historical need. *Minne* was in the first place a secularization of the adoration of the Virgin Mary, in that the knight fixed his affections on a high-born lady who, like the Virgin, must be worshipped from afar. In addition it was a refinement of the ancient Germanic virtues of constancy and loyalty. The minnesinger speaks not only for himself, but for all knights when he recounts the pains of love. He emphasizes his ability, and theirs, to endure suffering by portraying his passion and frustration as limitless. He demonstrates his, and their undying loyalty by insisting that, although the lady does not in the least reward his affection, he will remain faithful to her forever. In most of the minnesongs the lady is sketched quite indistinctly, for actually the song is less about her than about *minne* itself, and is less a praise of love than an exaltation of self, a demonstration of nobility in suffering.

The minnesong, as well as the courtly lyric in general, was a highly formalized art. The goals toward which the poet strove were not so much originality of character or content, but of form and symmetry. He sought not the unusual, but new arrangements of what was already familiar: new metrical patterns, new methods of employing symbols and metaphors, new ways of presenting conventional situations.

The earliest of the knightly singers antedate the concept of *minne* as well as certain other aspects of chivalry, and their love songs do not differ appreciably from those of the *Spielleute*. However, the courtly lyric developed rapidly and within a generation the simple and naive songs of a Kürenberg or Dietmar had become the highly sophisticated verse of the classical minnesong.

The first of the aristocratic singers was a Knight of Kürenberg, probably a member of the family which occupied Kürnberg Castle, near Linz, Austria, during the twelfth century. Kürenberg's songs were composed about the middle of the century or soon after and are, therefore, among the very earliest love songs in the German language. Of the fifteen stanzas which have been preserved, twelve consist of two sets of rhymed couplets with long lines divided by caesuras. Frequently there is assonance instead of pure rhyme. The remaining three stanzas have an additional short line; however, some scholars believe this was not a part of the original stanza, but added later by someone other than the author. The prevailing structure of Kürenberg's stanzas is closely related to that of Old Germanic epic verse and is the same as that employed in the twelfth century epic poem, 'The Song of the Nibelungs.' Kürenberg's songs are pre-courtly and have nothing to do with the concept of *minne*. They probably resemble in form and spirit the best of the *Spielmann* lyrics of his day. There is a charming simplicity of language and feeling in them and a portrayal of natural, naive emotions. In about half of his verse the speaker is a woman. She is not the cold and distant lady of the minnesong, but warm and affectionate, eager to love and be loved.

As the earliest of the knightly poets Kürenberg was in several respects an innovator. In the first stanza which appears here he introduces the message and the messenger into German love verse. The idea, of course, comes from the epistle, which was the most popular type of love poem in Medieval Latin literature. That Kürenberg, and the minnesingers who followed him, should use an oral message rather than a letter to convey the sentiments of the lover is indicative of the shift from a primarily written to a primarily oral art, from a literary to a performance tradition, which occurred when German replaced Latin as a medium for lyrical expression. In stanzas three and seven below the necessity for secrecy and the fear of 'spies' are expressed, both of which are conceits borrowed from Medieval Latin verse that later became standard conventions of the minnesong. The last two stanzas belong together and form Kürenberg's best known song. Although the subject is a falcon, the song also tells us something of the lonely woman in whose mouth the lines are placed. She sees the contrast between the freedom of the falcon and her own position, separated from the one she loves. This use of the falcon symbol is repeated frequently in the minnesong, and in later German verse as well.

THE LOVELIEST OF WOMEN

(Aller wîbe wunne)

The loveliest of women   is still a little maid;
I'll send to her a message   in words of fondest praise,
I'd go myself, if certain   it would not cause her woe.
I wonder if she loves me;   no maid has pleased me so.

DEAR AND LOVELY WOMAN

(Wîp vil schône)

Dear and lovely woman,   journey now with me,
happiness and sorrow   I will share with thee.
So long as I have hold on life   so faithful will I prove
and grant thee all, and ever   be constant in my love.

THE MISTY STAR OF EVENING

(Der tunkel sterne)

The misty star of evening   glows and quickly dies,
as does your glance, fair lady,   when it meets my eyes.

And then you turn your face away   toward anyone you see,
so none can guess the secret   you share with only me.

WHEN I AM IN MY NIGHTGOWN

(Swenne ich stân al eine)

When I am in my nightgown,   alone and lonely here
and when I think of thee,   my noble cavalier,
my color turns to crimson   as the rosebud on the thorn,
and then within my bosom   such sad desire is born.

TO BE TOWARD FRIENDS A STRANGER

(Vil lieber vriund vremden)

To be toward friends a stranger   causes grief and pain:
who's ever true to loved ones   merits praise and fame.
I like this common saying.
Go, bid him still be faithful   now as in the past,
remind him of what we promised   when I saw him last.

WHY SPEAK OF COMING SORROW

(Wes mansdu mich leides)

Why speak of coming sorrow,   thou most dear to me?
That we should part forever,   that must never be.
If I should lose thy favor,
then would I let the people   clearly understand
how little is my pleasure   in any other man.

CARE WILL CHANGE TO SORROW

(Leit machet sorge)

Care will change to sorrow   every fond delight:
I became acquainted   with a handsome knight;

that they drove him forth from me,   the spies with evil art,
has robbed me of my joy   and left a heavy heart.

LAST NIGHT I STOOD, MY LADY

(Jo stuont ich nechtint spâte)

Last night I stood, my lady   beside your bed,
but did not dare to wake you up,   and left.
'God's wrath be on your head,'   the lady swore,
'what did you think I was,   an angry boar?'

I RAISED MYSELF A FALCON

(Ich zôch mir einen valken)

I raised myself a falcon   longer than a year.
I tamed and made him gentle   as I would have him be,
and wove among his feathers   slender golden strands,
he mounted up toward heaven   and flew to other lands.

I later saw the falcon   flying swift and strong,
and fastened to his talons   he wore a silken thong,
his wings and coat of feathers   gleamed with red and gold.
May God bring those together   who gladly would their lovers
hold.

A slightly younger contemporary of Kürenberg's was Meinloh
of Söflingen, a South German town (now a suburb of the city
of Ulm) which was once the home of knights who were vassals
of the Counts of Dillingen. Only one member of the family of
the poet has been mentioned in the records of the time, perhaps a
son or grandson who appears in a document of 1240. Apparently
the family died out before 1270, for in that year the ancestral
castle of the Söflingens became a convent.

To Söflingen have been attributed twelve stanzas in all, each a
complete poem. He employs three *Töne*. Nine of his stanzas

consist of six long lines with caesuras and parallel rhyme and one unrhymed short line, which is called an 'orphan.' Two other stanzas are like the first group, except that they have no orphan. The twelfth stanza has four couplets instead of three and has an orphan. These structural patterns are early ones and could hardly have been in use after 1170. Also in other respects do the stanzas indicate an early date of composition. The language is still simple and the lovers are guided by their passions, not by the sophisticated rules of a social game. Like Kürenberg, Söflingen composed 'lady's songs,' that is, songs which express the words and sentiments of women. This in itself dates him, for the lady's song (*Frauenlied*) appears only rarely in the later love songs. One can see some Provençal influence in the work of Söflingen and the beginning of the courtly minnesong. Particularly in the fourth stanza below, one notes the concept of *Frauendienst* (service to ladies) and that the word 'virtue' has already taken on a chivalric meaning. Still, these are not yet minnesongs and the lovers need not bewail their sad fate, for they are usually well rewarded for their endeavors.

MY EYES HAVE SEEN AND CHOSEN

(Mir erwelten mîniu ougen)

My eyes have seen and chosen   for me a handsome youth
and other women envy   my fortune but, in truth,
I only seek to show him   that I am sweet and kind
and to this end give over   my heart and all my mind.
Whoever held his favor   before he was my own
has lost him with good reason,
yet I'll feel only sorrow   to see her stand alone.

WOE THEN TO THE GOSSIPS

(Sô wê den merkaeren)

Woe then to the gossips!   They show their evil will
by spreading wicked rumors,   although I've done no ill.

They think they'll spoil our friendship   by whispering about.
That I am still his sweetheart   they'll have no cause for doubt;
but God shall be my witness,   with him I've never lain.
Although my sense be blinded,
no other man could ever   cause love for him to wane.

I SAW THE SUMMER'S HERALDS

(Ich sach boten des sumeres)

I saw the summer's heralds   and they were flowers so red.
Do you know, lovely lady,   of what a noble said?
He offered you his service,   none else has pleased him so.
His heart is sad since leaving   you not so long ago.
Now you must raise his spirits   in this fair summertide,
for he will be dejected
till you at last embrace him   while lying by his side.

I KNOW JUST WHY I LOVE HER

(Ich bin holt einer frowen)

I know just why I love her,   this lady I adore,
since I began to serve her   she pleases me more and more.
She's dearer, ever dearer   to me as days go by,
she's fairer and still fairer: my love I can't deny.
She owns the highest virtue   and praises honor in men.
Were love of her to kill me,
and I then rejoin the living,   I'd woo the lady again.

I HAVE HEARD A STORY

(Ich hân vernomen)

I have heard a story   and it has thrilled my very heart,
for he has come to visit   who'll cause my sorrow to depart,
that I shall not be troubled   by longing and dejection.

Admonished by his virtue   I must be fast in my affection.
I think about him often,   the youth of whom they tell,
so may his coming bless me   who serves the ladies all so well.

The most gifted of the early knight-singers was Dietmar von
Aist, a poet whose songs belong to the best in German literature.
Dietmar was a member of a noble Austrian family whose castle
stood on the Alt-Aist Mountain near the Enns River. He is
mentioned in various documents from 1139 to 1169 and in a
document of 1171 is spoken of as already deceased. Dietmar's
work shows a much greater variety of forms and themes than
does that by Kürenberg and Meinloh, a fact which has caused
some scholars to speculate as to whether all of the stanzas
attributed to Dietmar are actually by the same man. However,
it is probable that they are and that the author, composing over
perhaps a twenty-year period, developed more complex *Töne*
and increasingly reflected Romance influences which may have
come to him by way of *Spielleute* and goliards. The stanzas
which are obviously the earliest have a naive, folk-like nature
and parallel, often impure, rhyme. They are lady's songs. The
later songs have more complicated structures, some have alter-
nating rhyme, and reveal something of the formalized and
sophisticated tone of the classical minnesong. However, even
in the later songs, Dietmar does not sing of *minne*, but of a purely
natural love, and it is still the lady rather than the knight who
seeks to win favor with the loved one, who weeps for loneliness,
and who shows devotion and constancy.

   Two types of songs appear for the first time in German
literature with Dietmar: the alternating song and the dawn song.
In the former the lovers speak in turn: perhaps to each other,
perhaps to a messenger, perhaps only to themselves, in the later
alternating songs a third person, usually a watchman, also has
his say. The dawn song is a particular kind of alternating song:
the lovers have spent the night in each others' arms and now
pour forth their grief that they must part. It is interesting that
the dawn song, although it assumes that love has been consum-
mated and, therefore, goes contrary to the pure concept of *minne*,

remained popular throughout the history of the minnesong. Perhaps the reason for this is that the song is never of the joys of love, but of the sorrow of parting, and, therefore, preserves the basic idea of the cult of *minne*—the revelation of nobility of character through suffering and renunciation.

In the first of the poems below, 'Gay Summer's Bliss, Goodbye,' Dietmar has grouped his nature symbols together at the beginning of the stanza to form a 'nature introduction,' a poetic device which was used previously in Medieval Latin verse and later became very popular among the minnesingers. It served them as a means of establishing a particular mood, sad or gay, for the narrative to follow. In the next song, 'A Lady Stood Alone,' one finds again Kürenberg's symbol of freedom, the falcon. The third song, 'Page of my Languishing Sweetheart,' belongs to Dietmar's later period. It is an alternating song in which a knight and his far-away sweetheart in turn address a messenger. The influence of Medieval Latin verse is seen particularly in the salutation which introduces each of the messages.

GAY SUMMER'S BLISS, GOODBYE

(So wôl dir sumerwunne)

Gay summer's bliss, goodbye!
The bird's sweet song has died,
the linden's leaves are gone,
the fading year beyond
will make these fair eyes weary.
My love, hear this entreaty:
all other charms
avoid, and other arms.
The moment that you met me
your manly form impressed me,
I thought you wondrous fair—
so, lover dear, beware!

A LADY STOOD ALONE

(Es stuont ein frouwe aleine)

A lady stood alone
and looked out on the plain
and waited for her love;
she saw a falcon high above.
'Lucky falcon there on high!
Whither you wish you fly;
you choose from the forest trees
whichever one you please.
So I too have done:
I chose myself a man,
my two eyes did agree.
But charming women envy me.
Oh, why do they set their snares?
I never wanted a lover of theirs.'

PAGE OF MY LANGUISHING SWEETHEART

(Seneder friundinne bote)

'Page of my languishing sweetheart,   now say to the lady fair,
my absence from her has caused me grief   and sorrow beyond
compare.
I would rather have her love
than songs of all the birds above.
Now that we must stay so long apart
deepest sadness seizes all my heart.'
'Just say to the knight so noble,   that I do wish him well,
and bid him ever be full of joy,   and all his fears dispel.
I so often for him must pine,
which sorely troubles this heart of mine.
All I see about me gives me pain,
of this I'll speak when once we meet again.'

In the first dawn song of German literature, 'Still Sleeping,
Handsome Knight,' Dietmar well illustrates the painstaking

symmetry which even the earliest minnesongs display. It employs a three-part structure that consists of two *Stollen*, which together make up what is called the rising song (*Aufgesang*), and the falling song (*Abgesang*). The two *Stollen* have identical metrical patterns and are sung to the same melody, while the falling song presents a new pattern and tune. This is a basic structure which is used in many, if not most, of the minnesongs throughout the history of the genre. In Dietmar's song the first eight lines make up the rising song with its two *Stollen*; the last four lines form the falling song. In the first *Stollen*, in which a lady speaks, the word 'sleeping' in the first line parallels 'Awake! Awake!' in the second line, while objects of nature, the birds and the linden tree, appear in parallel in the third and fourth lines. These two symbols of happiness contrast with the sorrow implied in the first half of the *Stollen*.

In the second *Stollen* (lines five to eight), in which a knight is speaking, it will be noted that the first two lines parallel the first two lines of the first *Stollen*. 'I slept gently' answers 'Still sleeping?' and 'you give the alarm' corresponds to 'Take flight!' The first two lines of the second *Stollen* also contrast with each other as 'love' contrasts with 'sorrow' in the following line. Both emotions are resolved in the concept of service and duty which is presented in the last line of the second *Stollen* (line eight).

The concluding four lines, the falling song, present the real theme of the poem, which is the lament of the lady at the departure of her lover. The rising song merely sets the scene for this outpouring of sorrow. Similar symmetrical patterns are found in many other courtly songs, both minnesongs and *Sprüche*.

STILL SLEEPING, HANDSOME KNIGHT

(Slafestu, vriedel ziere)

'Still sleeping, handsome knight?
Awake! Awake! Take flight!
A bird in all its finery

warns us from the linden tree.'
'I slept gently on your arm,
and now, sweetheart, you give the alarm;
but love must have its sorrow too,
what you command I'll quickly do.'
The lady then began to moan,
'You ride and leave me all alone.
When will you ever return to me?
With you my joys and pleasures flee.'

The stanza, 'Yonder on the Linden Tree,' is an alternating song
which voices first the thoughts of the knight and then those of
his far-away sweetheart. In the song one can see how objects
of nature have become specific artistic conventions. The linden
is summer, the bird is life and happiness, the rose is love. The
knight is reminded of the lady who combines these character-
istics. In the second *Stollen* the lady presents the same symbols
in connection with the knight, whom she has not seen for so
long. The over-all symbolism is, of course, the summer-winter,
joy-sorrow pattern which can be seen in a great number of
courtly songs.

The second song below, 'The Winter Such a Time Would Be,'
appears in one manuscript under the name of Heinrich von
Veldeke, but is generally attributed to Dietmar. The song has
two characteristics which connect it with the later minnesong:
alternating rhyme in place of rhymed couplets and a love plaint
by a man instead of a woman. Dietmar uses this *Ton* for several
other poems. It is possible that it was written to fit a tune by
the Provençal singer, Bernart de Ventadorn. Although there
was little direct contact between Austria and Provence at the
time that Dietmar was composing, the songs of Bernart were
widely known and could have been transmitted to Dietmar by
a *Spielmann* or wandering cleric. During the generation directly
following that of Dietmar it became a rather common practice
for German poets to use Provençal and French melodies.

(Ûf der linden obene)

'Yonder on the linden tree   there sang a merry little bird.
Its voice rang out at the forest's edge   and then my heart, by
memory stirred,
returned to a place that it once knew.   I saw the roses gently
blow;
they bring a host of thoughts about   a certain lady that I know.'
'It seems at least a thousand years   since in my lover's arms
I lay,
and I am not to blame that he   has left me now for many a day.
Since then I've seen no flowers bloom   and heard no bird's
enchanting song,
since then my joy has been short-lived,   my pain and sorrow
all too long.'

THE WINTER SUCH A TIME WOULD BE

(Der winter waere mir ein zît)

The winter such a time would be
of wondrous happiness and bliss
were a certain lady here with me
to still my yearning with a kiss.
I'd bless the longest winter night,
if I could spend it by her side,
but now so wretched is my plight
with sorrow that I cannot hide.

As one might expect, fewer of the early courtly singers remained
anonymous than was the case with the wandering *Spielleute* and
goliards. Nevertheless, a great many songs by members of the
lower nobility, both of the earlier and later Middle High German
period, cannot be identified as to author. The composers of the
two songs below were certainly contemporaneous with Küren-

berg, Meinloh and Dietmar; the long, divided lines, the use (in the originals) of impure rhyme, and the fact that they are lady's songs are sufficient proof of this. The songs most resemble those of Dietmar, particularly in their use of certain standardized devices: the general relationship between the mood of nature and the mood of the singer, the use of the red rose as a symbol of love and the bird as a symbol of joy, and the vaguely sketched but ominous enemies of true love. Although one may find these devices in the Latin verse of the time and earlier, this is in itself no proof of influence, since such elements appear in the love poetry of all lands and places. However, that they should constantly reappear in a similar manner throughout the courtly verse of the medieval period is evidence of the development of a well-known and generally accepted literary tradition.

NOTHING IS SO GOOD

(Mich dunket niht sô guotes)

Nothing is so good   and worthy, I contend,
as are gleaming roses   and the favor of my friend.
The little birds now sing
in the woods, delight   to many hearts they bring,
but, if my young man doesn't come,   I'll have no joys of
spring.

THE LINDEN TREE AGAIN

(Diu linde ist an dem ende)

The linden tree again   has long been thin and bare.
My lover hates me, I suffer   for what I could never share.
Unfaithful women are many   and they affect his mind;
God knows the truth, that I   am loyal to him and kind.
They only try to deceive   the inexperienced men:
alas, I fear for his youth!   I'll have naught but sorrow again.

5

INTERMEDIARIES BETWEEN PROVENCE
AND GERMANY

The three chief representatives of the early singers of the German nobility—Kürenberg, Söflingen, and Dietmar—lived in South Germany and Austria and began to compose at about the middle of the century. They were a part of a Southern flowering of lyric verse which, in spite of some Romance influence, was largely native and was doubtless closely related to the popular songs of the non-aristocratic public. The three chief intermediaries between Provençal and German songs—Friedrich von Hausen, Heinrich von der Veldeke, and Rudolf von Fenis—lived, as one might expect, close to the boundaries of France and Provence, and began to compose about twenty years later. In their work the Romance element is sometimes not completely assimilated and one can often distinguish between Romance and German features. The chivalric aspects of their verse are more French-Provençal than native and introduce an entire terminology of poetic expressions and courtly ideas. Since all of them composed some lyrics to Romance tunes, their metrical patterns also were strongly influenced by the older and more sophisticated art to the west. The *Töne* became much more complex than those of the South German-Austrian song, having lines of varying length and intricate rhyme patterns.

Friedrich von Hausen was a prominent man of his day, was known at the imperial court, and mentioned rather frequently in contemporary documents. He was born in the Rhineland, possibly in the vicinity of Mainz, about the middle of the century. He is first mentioned together with his father in 1171 and a second time in 1175 when he accompanied the Archbishop of Mainz to Italy, which country he visited again in 1186 as a part of the retinue of Emperor Friedrich I (Barbarossa). The following year he was in France and present at an historically important meeting between the Emperor and King Philipe-Auguste. Two years later, in 1189, he departed with the Emperor on the Third Crusade and died in battle against the Turks in 1190, about a month before the death of Barbarossa.

Because of its position at the junction of the Rhine and Main Rivers, Mainz in the twelfth century was an important center of trade and of cultural exchange between the German-speaking and French-speaking peoples. Here, as well as on his travels to Italy and France, Hausen became acquainted with Provençal songs and with the chivalric concepts, themes, and conceits which they expressed. Although he was the first of the minnesingers to be strongly influenced by the troubadors, he was not merely an imitator, for there remains much of the native song in his verse and much that is distinctly his own. His language and his *Töne* are relatively simple compared both to those of the troubadors and those of the later minnesingers. But that which is most characteristic of Hausen's poetry results from his strong religious feeling and his effort to establish an inner relationship between religion and *minne*. He rejects the frank desire for sexual satisfaction which appears in Dietmar and veils erotic elements with abstract expressions which are more transcendental than the formulas of the troubadors. With Hausen beauty exists as the creation of God, and it, therefore, cannot be sinful for man to love beauty, but physical attractiveness must be accompanied by virtue if it is to be beautiful. In his songs he attempts, not always to his own complete satisfaction, to combine *minne* and religion to a Christian ethic.

Fifty-five of Hausen's stanzas are extant. In them can be seen the influence of Bernart de Ventadorn, Folquet de Marseille, and Conon de Bethune. The alternating song, 'That I Should Go Away,' appears to be a contrafact composed to a melody by Bernart de Ventadorn. In it Hausen sings neither of purely physical passion nor of *minne*, but of what we call 'true love,' which is temporarily frustrated by deceivers and the 'guardians.'

With the latter the poet introduces new characters into the minnesong, but the identity of the guardians here, as also in the later minnesong, remains vague. It is interesting that, even though it is generally assumed that the heroine of the minnesong is a married woman, none of the minnesingers ever refers to a jealous husband. In the song, 'The Sweetest Words Which Ever I,' appears for the first time in German verse the most popular theme of the minnesingers—the unrequited love of a knight for a lady. This was a part of the Provençal tradition from which he drew. Another influence of the troubadors can be seen in the conscious use of a polystrophic structure in the second poem and in the virtuosity of recurring rhyme in both the first and second poems. It is possible that 'The Sweetest Words Which Ever I' is a contrafact of a song by Chrétien de Troyes. The third song below, 'She Can Never Say of Me,' has a simpler rhyme scheme than the first two, but a more complicated rhythmical pattern, consisting of dimeter, tetrameter, and pentameter lines. It is interesting, however, that Hausen, for all his sophistication of form, still frequently uses assonance instead of pure rhyme, as is indicated in the translation by the rhyming of 'sleep' and 'greet.' It is possible that the final stanza of this song refers to Hausen's intention to join a crusade. The song was probably composed to a melody by Folquet de Marseille.

THAT I SHOULD GO AWAY

(Deich von der guoten schiet)

'That I should go away
and give her no farewell,
although I wished to stay,
is grief I cannot tell.
They led me thus astray
who would my love dispel:
I hope they get their pay
from him who rules in hell;
there may they ever dwell.'

'These guardians of mine
would rescue me from woe.
I see their foul design,
they'll not succeed, I know.
They'd sooner turn the Rhine
to empty in the Po
and make the streams combine
before I'd let him go
who always loved me so.'

THE SWEETEST WORDS WHICH EVER I

(Diu süezen wort hânt mir getân)

The sweetest words which ever I
have heard from people I have known
are all of her, and that is why
my love for her has always grown.
My other cares are small, I own,
compared to that for which I sigh.
In all the world beneath the sky,
God knows, I love her alone.
My suit deserves a fair reply.

Of all the women God has dressed
with shapely form and pleasing air
He's granted her His very best;
there's none so charming, none so fair.
What though my love is sometimes care,
with joy it often fills my breast.
My life would then be fully blessed,
If she would rue her sins, forbear
to pain me till I'm sore distressed.

Whatever pleasures God has made
are not increased through her for me,
my sorrow she has not allayed,
nor given answer to my plea.

A hardened heart has let her be
so cruel that she's never swayed
by all the grief which I've displayed
and cannot longer bear. Thus she
my love and loyalty repaid.

SHE CAN NEVER SAY OF ME

(Si darf mich des zîhen niet)

She can never say of me,
I did not love her tenderly.
The truth of this she ought to recognize,
not close her eyes.
I often suffered such distress
that I would say 'Good morning,' I confess,
when eve was nigh.
So lost in thoughts of her was I
that I would often walk as if in sleep
and never hear a word when friends would greet.

I served a lady with heart and sword,
but all my love brought no reward.
And still I speak of her with only praise,
although her gaze
has never yet been turned to me in kindness.
I fancied I was free of passion's blindness,
but, still in bands,
my heart sought favor from her hands,
which it has never gotten, I must say.
I'll serve Him now who will my love repay.

From love I've only known despair
and happiness was something rare.
But, though my heart with bitter pain was stirred,
no one has heard
my lips a single censure tell,
for I have always spoken women well.

66

Still I regret
that I could God so long forget.
I'll serve Him first of all and only then
shall I to ladies yield my heart again.

The tripartite structure of two *Stollen* and a falling song did not disappear with the development of songs of more than one stanza, but continued to be used by many, if not most of the lyric poets of medieval Germany. Hausen, however, used it only infrequently. In the poem, 'Now and Then I Ponder,' the stanzas can be divided into rising song and falling song. However, if the verses were written to a melody by Guiot de Provins, as has been claimed, then the stanzas are not tripartite, for the music does not repeat within the stanza. The song is the traditional lover's plaint, so popular at this time in Provence. The following song, 'Alas, My Heart is Sore,' is also a traditional plaint, but has some characteristics which are especially typical of Hausen: kindliness and good sense. His kindliness causes him to wish the lady in the song happiness, although she has not returned his affection; his good sense makes him feel that his heart is most foolish to choose one who will not love him. In effect, he questions the basic principle, renunciation, of courtly love. The personification of love in the last stanza is a part of the Romance influence. One reason Hausen does not criticize the lady is that he feels Love (Venus) itself is to blame. The verses of 'Alas, My Heart is Sore' were probably composed to an extant melody by an anonymous trouvère.

In the third song below, 'I See the Wonders God Can Do,' Hausen introduces into the German courtly lyric a device, the refrain, which was in common usage not only in Romance song, but also in Latin hymns, and probably also in the German folk song. During a performance the audience was expected, of course, to join the soloist in singing the refrain. The last song is the oldest crusade song the composer of which is known. For one of Hausen's religious nature the obligation to support the Third Crusade would have been unequivocal, even if he had not been so closely associated with Friedrich Barbarossa, the leader of the crusade. It is characteristic of Hausen that he appeals neither to love of adventure nor to hate of the enemy, but to duty to God.

(Ich denke under wîlen)

Now and then I ponder
o'er that which I'd be saying
if she were here with me.
It shortens roads I wander
to let my thoughts go straying
to her with plaint and plea.
But when the people see
my face, they think I'm playing,
so gay I seem to be
to hide my misery.

Had I not undertaken
a love so high as ours,
I might perhaps find aid.
I did it when forsaken
by sense, now care devours
each happy plan I've made.
For loyalty has swayed
my will and overpowers
a heart that would have strayed
when hopes had been betrayed.

Whatever may betide me
one joy I'll always treasure
and never let it go:
to dream of her beside me,
though distant lands I measure.
This comfort she'll bestow.
If she would have it so,
the greater is my pleasure;

no other man I know
such constancy would show.

ALAS, MY HEART IS SORE

(Mir ist daz herze wunt)

Alas, my heart is sore
and has been sick for many a year,
'twas not a fool before
it learned to know a lady here,
but should the king himself appear
and place a kiss or more
on lips which I adore,
he'd swear, he'd never known their peer.

My heart I gave away
to one who ranks among the best,
and would receive my pay,
if she would grant me one request.
But though my suit has not been blessed,
though she no love display,
my hope is that she may
have more of joy than all the rest.

Who better could relieve
my pain than could the lady fair
who taught me how to grieve
with sorrow none can see nor share.
Still I deserve the pain I bear:
such hopes I should not weave.
If Love can thus deceive,
then every lover must beware.

69

I SEE THE WONDERS GOD CAN DO

(Ich sihe wol daz got wunder kan)

I see the wonders God can do
of lovely works in human form.
My lady's showed, when He was through,
that He forgot no single charm.
The grief she causes me, the harm,
that will I bear, and gladly too,
so I may stay and in her arms
have all my fondest dreams come true.
What e'er she does, my love shall see
that she'll not soon be rid of me.

Let her not think that I bestow
my love in passing or in play.
While still a child and long ago,
to her I gave my heart away
and have been faithful since the day
I first began to love her so.
My heart, still subject to her sway,
eternal loyalty will show.
What e'er she does, my love shall see
that she'll not soon be rid of me.

THEY SEEK TO ESCAPE FROM DEATH AND PAIN

(Sie wânent dem tôde entrunnen sin)

They seek to escape from death and pain
who take no part in God's crusade,
but this I know: their hope is vain
and they have but themselves betrayed.
Who took the cross and gave no aid
will find in death his error plain
and stand before the gate, dismayed,
which opens wide for God's true thane.

Heinrich von Veldeke was also born in the Rhineland. He was a member of a family of minor nobility which had held properties in the Limburg region of present-day Belgium. About the year 1170 he was living at the Court of the Duke of Cleve, where he composed 'The Legend of Saint Servatius,' a long poem adapted from a Latin source. Sometime during the next ten years he moved to the court of Count Hermann of Thuringia, a famous patron of the minnesong. It was at the latter's castle at Neuenberg that Veldeke composed his best-known work, *Eneit*, the first of the German courtly epics. Although the poem is based on the *Aeneid*, the immediate source was not Vergil's work, but that of a Frenchman, Benoit de Sainte-Maure. In 1184 Veldeke was the chief musical performer at the imperial festival at Mainz, arranged by Emperor Friedrich I on the occasion of the knighting of his two sons. It is estimated that as many as 50,000 people—nobles, knights, and minstrels—from all points of the empire may have attended the festival, the most grandiose and colorful spectacle of medieval times. Veldeke became at once the most famous and influential poet in Germany. His influence was exerted in the direction of pure rhyme, regular rhythm, and a stricter and more artistic form. He is praised in works by several of his contemporaries, especially by Gottfried von Strassburg who, in the courtly epic, *Tristan and Isolde*, names him as the one who grafted the first twig in the German language from which the branches sprang and the blossoms came. Certainly at the court of Hermann (who was reared in France) and probably before then, Veldeke had heard Provençal and French singers and had assimilated their art and chivalric ideas. In addition, Veldeke was a highly educated man who read French and Latin and was, therefore, able to exploit non-German sources. It is with him that the cult of *minne* and the minnesong proper begins. *Minne* becomes the greatest of aesthetic and cultural values and the source of all virtues. Indeed, in the verse of Veldeke, in contrast to that of Hausen, one might say that the ethic of *minne* replaces the Christian ethic.

Veldeke's songs have neither the naive charm and frank sensuousness of Dietmar nor the depth of feeling of Hausen. His

71

characters are involved in a pleasant social game which he describes in lighthearted, sometimes even humorous language. Indeed, for all of his stylized conceits there is something of the freshness of the folksong in some of his verse. And though he uses sophisticated metrical patterns one gets the impression of simple elegance rather than ostentatious artistry. Veldeke depicts nature to a greater extent than did his predecessors and, although much of his nature description is formal convention, sometimes one feels that it is more than this. Veldeke composed both single strophic and polystrophic songs, sometimes to Romance tunes. In adapting the Provençal ten-syllable line to German tetrameter he was the inventor of the German dactyl, although he uses it infrequently. He was also the first to employ the run-on line to any extent.

Veldeke died before 1210. Fifty-five stanzas of his verse survive, but none of his melodies, except a few which may have been borrowed as contrafacts from trouvère songs. Although Veldeke composed his songs in the Low German of his Limburg homeland, they appear in the manuscripts only in High German. However, scholars have translated them back into their original form, which is that used below the following titles.

Veldeke sings of love, but usually as a personification or abstraction, rather than as a personal emotion. Sometimes he cannot restrain the impulse to poke fun at it, as he does in the third stanza of 'So Kind is She and Oh, So Fair' where he intimates that, although *minne* is fine, money is even better. He sings of the joys of spring and the weary desolation of winter. He composes traditional lover's plaints as well as lady's songs. One of his most unusual songs belongs to the latter group. In literally hundreds of poems the minnesingers tell of love-sick knights who complain that the object of their affections grants them no favors, but Veldeke's 'I'm Glad that Each Succeeding Day' is perhaps the only song in which the other side of the picture appears. Here the lady complains of a lover who was not satisfied with a purely Platonic relationship and expresses her annoyance in a somewhat humorous vein. This poem was apparently written to music by Gace Brulé.

I BEG THEE, LOVE, WHOSE YOKE I DON

(Die minne bite ich ende man)

I beg thee, Love, whose yoke I don,
who has captured me as a prize,
that thou mayest hurry my sweetheart on
to better reward my sighs.
For should I fare as doth the swan,
who sings his melody and dies,
I would pay too much for the joy I've won.

TRISTAN, NOT FROM HIS DESIRE

(Tristrant moeste sonder danc)

Tristan, not from his desire,
served the queen with true devotion,
subject to a lover's fire
less than to a magic potion.
Therefore should my lady thank
me, for though I never drank
such a brew, my heart's emotion
equals that from witch's wine.
Thing of beauty, truth and duty,
grant that I be thine
and that thou be mine!

WHEN THE SEASONS THUS DECREE

(Swenn die tîd alsô gestât)

When the seasons thus decree
that grass may green and flowers bloom,
my heart will then at last be free
from all that burdened it with gloom.
The birds would rejoice, and not alone,
if summer always would remain.
Though the world were all my own,
the winter still would cause me pain.

73

(Sît die sonne her liehten skîn)

When the summer sun is chill
and before the winter cowers,
when the songs of birds are still
in the field and woodland bowers,
sadness then my heart will fill
for it won't be long until
winter shows to us its powers.
In the blossoms we shall see
brilliant shade
pale and fade;
this will bring to me
no joy, but misery.

(Sî is so gût ende ouch so scône)

So kind is she and Oh, so fair
whom I have often praised ere now,
had I the crown of Rome to wear
I'd gladly place it on her brow.
'Behold, he's mad!' some folks would vow.
That she regard me is my prayer;
I know, if she is still as dear,
what I would do, if she were near,
but she is there, and I am here.

When she desired, she brought to me
so much of pleasure and delight
that I rejoice in memory
and all the joys of love recite.
For since I saw how she at night
could fool the watch as cleverly
as hounds by hares are oft deceived,

74

of all my fears I've been relieved,
nor for my father's son have grieved.

I'd rather have her for my own
and have a thousand marks to hold
and a chest with many a precious stone,
finely wrought from burnished gold,
than see myself grow sick and old
afar from her and all alone.
Of that she can be really sure
and in this trust may rest secure,
that it's a truth which will endure.

I'M GLAD THAT EACH SUCCEEDING DAY

(Ich bin vrô sint ons die dage)

'I'm glad that each succeeding day
which comes is longer and more bright.'
Thus spoke a woman without dismay,
but with an unrestrained delight.
'I thank my lucky stars at night
that I've a heart which none can sway
and that no feebleness can blight
nor steal my happiness away.

'There was a time, not long ago,
when I was courted by a man
to whom much kindness I did show,
which I shall grant no more, nor can,
since he so brazenly began
to ask for favors which, I know,
I sooner shall refuse him than
he'll ever get me to bestow.

'I thought him versed in courtly art
and that is why, I must confess,
I loved him once with all my heart,

but he's quite free of such finesse.
Still, I can bear his pain, I guess,
and little care how he may smart.
He thought he'd have a great success,
but he'll have little when we part.'

Rudolf II, Count of Fenis-Neuenberg and descendant of Burgundian kings, was born about the middle of the twelfth century and died in 1196. His ancestral estates included both German-speaking and Provençal areas. He was certainly bilingual and his verse shows familiarity with the songs of Provence. The eight of his minnesongs which survive were influenced by these songs with regard to metrics and content, especially by those of the Provençal bishop, Folquet de Marseille.

Structurally Fenis' verse is of particular interest in that it clearly illustrates the Romance origin of the German dactyl. It is melodious, but too impersonal and affected to be appealing and, though he uses some strikingly apt metaphors, what is best in his poetry inevitably turns out to be borrowed. His songs all deal with a languishing lover, but give us no picture of the beloved, for his plaints are directed to *minne* itself, rather than to a particular woman. For the first song below Fenis used a melody by Folquet, for the second a melody (and considerable content) by Gace Brulé, for the third song a melody by Folquet. The best of this last song lies in the skillful use of the moth-flame symbol, which, however, was also taken from Folquet. In general, Fenis is important as an intermediary, rather than as a poet in his own right.

THOUGH I MAY HAVE FANCIED
THAT LOVE WOULD SHOW

(Gewan ich ze minnen ie guoten wân)

Though I may have fancied that love would show
me favor, I've gained from it nothing but sorrow,
nor do I see how I shall profit tomorrow,

since I cannot have her nor let her go;
like one who has climbed up a tree that is shaking,
who cannot go higher for fear of it breaking
and can't make his way again down to the ground
and sits there for hours with fear and with quaking.

And I am like one who has fastened his heart
and his mind on a game that he plays till he loses
and then gives it up, but too late he so chooses.
So I, too, discovered, too late to depart
from the guile Love employed in the game she was playing.
She brought me to her, my disquiet allaying
with friendliest smiles, as a debtor does
who promises much, but has no thought of paying.

LOVE HAS COMMANDED THAT I SHOULD SING

(Minne gebiutet mir daz ich singe)

Love has commanded that I should sing,
and forbids me ever to complain,
though she no comfort nor hope may bring
that my song its fitting reward should gain.
She wishes that I should give my love away
where my devotion no heart can sway
and where faithfulness offers little as pay.
I strive to leave her service, but in vain.

This is my lot, that I cannot permit
my heart forever to renounce its claim.
It is my sorrow, that I've not the wit
to give up serving one who hates my name.
I'll cherish her still, whatever may befall,
loyalty keeps me always in thrall,
and in spite of the fact that its wages are small.
Though she is vexed, I'll love her just the same.

(Mit sange wânde ich mîne sorge krenken)

I fancied I could lighten grief by singing,
so now I sing to free my heart from care,
but with the music grievous thoughts come winging
and song can only lay my sorrow bare.
For Lady Love has caught me in her snare,
she gives the hope to which I've long been clinging
and I cannot escape her anywhere.

Since Love in such a manner would reward me,
that I should carry in my heart's recess
the one who can for pain delight afford me,
I'd be a fool should I not acquiesce.
But I shall let Love know of my distress,
for she who's acted so disdainful toward me
could lead me to the house of Happiness.

I wonder at my constant adoration
and how she holds me when I'm far away,
for then I think, this is my consolation,
the sight of her my pain would soon allay.
'Were I with her!' it comforts me to say,
and hope at last to win her admiration,
but soon the hope increases my dismay.

When I'm with her I suffer more than ever,
like one who crowds too closely to a fire
and burns himself as pain for his endeavor,
her beauty pains me, yet it draws me nigher.
When I'm with her I feel my life expire,
but I would die indeed if we should sever,
for she is all my joy and my desire.

I feel the danger in those eyes so tender,
they charm me as the moth is charmed by light

and swiftly flies to perish in its splendor;
her beauty thus deludes my mind and sight.
My foolish heart has brought me to this plight
and, like the moth, is drawn in full surrender
toward flames which shall forever end its flight.

6

FOUR SINGERS OF THE
CLASSICAL PERIOD

The classical period of courtly song extended from about 1190 to about 1220. It was a period in which the best of the poets had fully assimilated the concepts, techniques, and themes of their Romance, goliard, and *Spielmann* contemporaries and predecessors to form a courtly lyric which was characteristically German. It was also a time when a specifically German chivalry existed that played a significant role in a courtly society which included many wealthy sponsors of the art of song. By now the courtly song had developed maturity without yet having lost its freshness of expression, and *minne* was still more than a mere poetic convention. Metrically the courtly lyric had achieved a smooth and skillful complexity which had not yet become ostentatious virtuosity, and courtly manners and the cult of *minne* had not become so exaggerated as to invite parody. The life described in the courtly song of the classical period may not have been the life that the nobility actually lived, but it was still poetically real to the audiences for which the artists composed and sang.

Little is known of the family or of the life of Heinrich von Morungen. A few traces of dialect in his verse point to middle Germany and it may well be that the Morungen Castle near Eisleben in Thuringia was his home. He was probably a vassal of the Margrave Dietrich IV of Meissen who ruled from 1195 to 1221. A document of about the year 1217 mentions the minnesinger and shows that he was transferring an annual stipend, received from the Margrave, to the St. Thomas Monastery in

Leipzig. He is referred to again in a document of 1218. However, since both documents indicate that Morungen was an old man at the time, it is quite certain that his verse was composed for the most part in the twelfth century. The fact that the earliest of his poems show the influence of Veldeke and that he himself influenced the young Walther von der Vogelweide would indicate that the majority of the works which have survived were composed in the nineties. The strong Provençal influence, the purity of rhyme, and a few connecting threads to other poets likewise point to this decade. It is probable that he spent the last years of his life in the St. Thomas Monastery which he had endowed. He died there in 1227. A fictional account of his life appears in the late medieval ballad, 'Vom edeln Möringer.'

The entire fanciful world of courtly love comes to life in the minnesongs of Morungen. He was a poet of great originality and imagination and in his hands the fixed conventions and stereotyped situations of the troubadours take on an immediacy and vitality that makes them live, even for the twentieth century reader. Although Morungen in general accepts the tradition of *minne*, he does not stray far from the real world about him, and there is always something very personal and human in his lovers' joys and sorrows, something very natural and genuine about their reactions to the situations in which he places them. There is a graceful charm and enchanting splendor in the wooing of the loved one, in the enjoyment of love's fulfillment, even in the melancholy or sharply bitter complaints. Above all, it is the richness and originality of his imagery that makes Morungen's verse distinctive. He has only the one theme, courtly love, but for him it was the power which ruled all and lent splendor and excitement to all being, it was the one certain value of life. And in the reactions of his knights and ladies to this value he shows himself to be a subtle psychologist as well as a master artist. In the diversity of their reactions lies the interesting variety of his art. Morungen's mood is generally a joyful and optimistic one, for all the momentary sadness or bitterness which his lovers may experience. It is enough to be able to live and to love.

In matters of structure Morungen has the true poet's talent for joining form and content. His metrical patterns are sometimes rather complex, but are always smooth and pliable. He achieves a total unity in his songs which is quite rare in the history of the minnesong, where the emphasis is usually on the stanza rather than on the poem as a whole. Rising song and falling song are joined by rhyme and rhythm patterns and there is close relationship and continuity from stanza to stanza. Often the end is rounded off by a return to the beginning. Rhymes are pure, double rhymes appear frequently, interior rhyme only rarely. Besides the influence of Provençal song and of Veldeke, there was possibly an influence of Ovid on his verse. At any rate, Morungen uses a number of Ovid's similes and metaphors.

In the first song which follows, a dawn song which is also an alternating song, the knight and lady are far apart and are recalling in alternate monologues the ecstasy and sorrow of parting. The first two stanzas describe the same situation as seen first by the knight, then by the lady; the second two stanzas are similarly parallel to each other. All four stanzas, however, are linked by simple but effective devices. The refrain at the end of the first stanza leads up to the 'daybreak' of the second stanza; the 'lay' at the end of the second stanza to the 'slept' at the beginning of the third stanza, etc. In the last stanza the naiveté of the lady is not only appealing, but was obviously intended to be also amusing, for Morungen had the rather rare talent of getting humor from his characters without making them appear ridiculous. The original is one of the most beautiful love songs, not only of medieval, but of all European literature.

In the song, 'What Lady is She,' the stanzas are not directly continuous in time, but represent separate stages of an unhappy love affair. In it one sees nothing of the clever playing with sentiment which characterizes most lover's laments. There is a stronger, almost violent emotion here and a bitterness which cries out for revenge, for the lover wishes his tomb to be a constant reminder of the cruelty of the lady who will cause his death.

The enduring force of love is the theme of the stanza, 'O Sweet, Benevolent Assassin.' The idea of a love so strong that its bonds cannot be broken in this life is a basic concept of courtly love. However, the minnesingers, for all their idealization of *minne*, were oriented essentially to matters of this world and only from Morungen do we learn of bonds of love so strong that not even death can break them. Morungen's ability to surprise us with a phrase is well illustrated in the unusual wording of the first line of the song and of the unexpected joyfulness of the last line.

Few love songs of any age have so well expressed the enthralling rapture of love as does 'On Such a Cloud of Joy as This.' The ecstasy, the pain, and the trembling, joyous fear are told in a deceptively simple language which, once more, is not without its trace of sympathetic humor. The rhyming in the original is handled so easily that one scarcely notices its complexity: *a b a b b a b*.

The last song given, 'Long I Brooded, Lost in Thought,' is somewhat inferior to most of Morungen's songs and possibly was not by him, although it appears in a manuscript under his name. It is, nevertheless, significant, for if it is Morungen's, it is the only one of his songs for which the melody is extant. The verses were composed to music by an anonymous trouvère.

OH! OH! WILL NEVERMORE THE GLOW

(Owê, sol aber mir iemer mê)

'Oh! Oh!
Will nevermore the glow
of that fair form as white
as newly-fallen snow
come to me through the night?
The sight deceived my eyes,
I thought I saw arise
the bright moon in the skies.
Then came the dawn!'

'Oh! Oh!
And will he never know
the daybreak here again,
nor watch the darkness go,

83

nor share my sorrow when
I cry: "Alas, it's day!"?
That he, too, used to say
when he beside me lay.
Then came the dawn!'

           'Oh! Oh!
A thousand times, it seems
she kissed me as I slept,
and, till I left my dreams,
how bitterly she wept.
But then I knew how best
to put her tears to rest;
she drew me to her breast.
Then came the dawn!'

           'Oh! Oh!
So many times has he
seen more than was his due
and quite uncovered me;
he wanted just to view
poor me, all bare and bright.
I wondered that my knight
so much enjoyed the sight.
Then came the dawn!'

WHAT LADY IS SHE

(Sach ieman die vrouwen)

What lady is she
whom one may see
in the window there?
Her beautiful face
and airy grace
can free me from care,
for she glows with the warmth of the rising sun
in the morning's early light.

84

Long was she hidden from sight
and dark was the night,
but now the world is all fair.

If someone is here
whose reason is clear
in this hour of gloom,
seek her who bereft me
of beauty and left me
to sorrow and doom,
and entreat her to hasten and soothe my grief
while life and breath remain.
For torments of passion and pain
I cannot restrain
are driving me to the tomb.

Then clearly make known
my fate on the stone
that covers my grave.
Tell of beauty adored
and a lover ignored,
that the knight or the knave
as he passes may learn from my sombre tale
of love that burns and rends.
There may he read how she sends
cold death to her friends,
so cruelly does she behave.

O SWEET, BENEVOLENT ASSASSIN

(Vil sûze senfte tôterinne)

O sweet, benevolent assassin,
why slay your love and me and cast aside
the hopes and tender ties that fasten
our hearts, and just to please your woman's pride?
Oh can you dream that, having killed me,
you then will wander free of my design?

No, no, so full your love has filled me
that evermore your soul is wed to mine.
Though here my heart may suffer sorrow
from one who lies so near it,
I tell you, soon, perhaps tomorrow,
my soul will love and serve you there,
a light and laughing spirit.

ON SUCH A CLOUD OF JOY AS THIS

(In sô hôher swebender wunne)

On such a cloud of joy as this
my soul has never sailed so high before.
I hover as on wings of bliss
with thoughts of only her whom I adore,
because her love unlocked the door
which leads into my inmost heart
and entered there for evermore.

All other raptures that remain
with this great happiness cannot compare.
Let earth and sky and wood and plain
with me a time of soaring gladness share.
For, filled with hope and freed from care,
and thrilled by dreams of ecstasy,
my joy is more than I can bear.

What all-entrancing words were those
which sounded, oh so sweetly, in my ear!
And what a gentle pain arose
to sink with joy into my bosom here,
where such delights did then appear,
such loving overcame me so,
that from my eye there fell a tear.

How happy was that sweet event!
How blissful was that hour, the fading night,

when lovely lips gave their consent
and spoke the word which made my heart so light
that I must tremble as in fright.
And even now love's power is so,
I know not how to praise her right.

LONG I BROODED, LOST IN THOUGHT

(Lanc bin ich geweset verdâht)

Long I brooded, lost in thought,
sad, unloved I long have been,
then to me the news was brought
which rejoiced my heart within.
Comfort I should win
from this lady of mine;
how could I now longer pine?
When her lips requite
my love with such delight
I can sorrow never more:
all my grief is o'er.

Although Hartmann von Aue appears in no official records, we
know something of him from his own works and from those of
his fellow writers. He was born about 1170, took part in the
Crusade of 1197-98, and died between the years 1210 and 1220.
He was a propertyless knight in the service of the Lords of Aue,
whose lands were near Rottenburg in Swabia. Hartmann was
highly regarded by the singers of his day, but less for his minne-
songs than for his long narrative poems. These include two
Arthurian romances, 'Erec' and 'Iwein,' both modeled after
works by Chrétien de Troyes; a legend of Saint Gregory, for
which Hartmann used a French and possibly also a Latin source;
and 'Poor Henry,' a didactic narrative, perhaps based on a family
tradition of his liege lords.

Sixty of Hartmann's stanzas are extant. Of these, fifty deal
with courtly love and the remainder are *Sprüche*. According to

one of Hartmann's contemporaries, he also composed at least one *Leich*, a lyric form which probably developed from the sequence, but this has been lost. It is assumed that the minne-songs were composed during the poet's youth. They are con-ventional in form and content, adhere closely to the ideal of courtly love, and show a strong Romance influence. The singer bewails the fact that his lady does not reward his service and is tormented with indecision and doubts. However, he must remain faithful in spite of all. In these lyrics Hartmann's passion and expression are restrained to the point that the songs some-times appear to be little more than mere reflections on the nature of chivalric love. His later, didactic verse is not only more mature and original, but also more spontaneous. A thinker and teacher here gives expression to matters with which he is per-sonally and deeply concerned. These are songs of melancholy sadness, of renunciation of worldy joys, of dedication to religious duty. Central to them is not the love of woman, but the love of God. There is some indication that Hartmann's insistence on loyalty and his strict interpretation of courtly love may have influenced the verse of Reinmar der Alte; his didactic verse, on the other hand, may have affected that of Walther von der Vogel-weide.

The first song below is from Hartmann's early period and is light-hearted, even exuberant. The dactylic rhythm is produced by his use of a French melody of Gace Brulé, which was com-posed for a ten-syllable line, for a tetrameter poem. The second song, 'No one is a Happy Man,' although ostensibly a love song, is actually a poem in which the vanity of all temporal joys and possessions is proclaimed. The lady who supposedly inspired the verses is almost forgotten. It has been suggested that Hart-mann composed the lines shortly before his departure on a crusade. The best known of the poet's songs is his crusade song, 'The Cross Demands a Guileless Mind.' He begins the song by setting spiritual standards for those who take the cross, the second stanza tells of the obligations and rewards of participation in a crusade, the third stanza is entirely personal and emphasizes the *vanitas mundi* theme, while the last stanza, likewise personal, is a tribute to his departed liege lord. The poem, 'The Wife Who

Sends Her Cherished Lord,' is also a crusade song and points out
the duties of the wives who are left behind.

I ALWAYS SHALL CHERISH THE DAY OF ALL DAYS

(Ich muoz von rehte den tac iemer minnen)

I always shall cherish the day of all days
when first I met her whose charm I extoll:
the loveliest manner and feminine ways.
I'm glad that I gave her my heart and my soul.
This cannot harm her and does me much good,
now I know God and the world as I should.
Since through her virtue my errors shall cease,
I hope that through her all my joys will increase.

I parted from her, and before I could tell
the lady how greatly my passion had grown.
Later a wonderful hour befell
as I discovered her walking alone.
When fate had led me to her I admire
and I had told her my fondest desire,
she was so kind—may God grant her renown!
She was and shall be forever my crown.

Although my body may sometimes take leave,
my heart and my longing must linger with her.
She may bring sadness and cause me to grieve,
yet drive from my heart all the troubles that stir;
from her I've my pleasure as well as my pain,
what she desires of me, she shall obtain,
when I am happy, it's due to her care
God keep her honor, and her, is my prayer.

NO ONE IS A HAPPY MAN

(Niemen ist ein saelic man)

No one is a happy man
upon this earth save he alone
who cherishes no secret plan
and seeks to make no joy his own.
Whose heart is free from longing care
which brings to many death's despair
who gained what to their heart was dear
and lived to see their treasures go.
To whom that life comes not so near
which I with sorrow learned to know,
for such has been my loss and woe.

It is a cheerless fate, which lends
its greeting to my every pain,
that I must always part from friends
with whom I gladly would remain.
My griefs from my devotion spring
but to the soul no profit bring,
else I should have a better pay
than to lament the constancy
which offers nothing but dismay
for her I never more shall see
who once so loved and cared for me.

THE CROSS DEMANDS A GUILELESS MIND

(Dem kriuze zimt wol reiner muot)

The cross demands a guileless mind
and chaste behavior:
so may salvation be combined
with worldly favor.
And it is not a little chain
for men as we

who o'er their bodies cannot gain
the mastery.
It wants not that one shirks
beneath it righteous works;
though wrought on coat of mail
within the heart it must prevail.

Then, knights, repay that which is due
and join the strife
for one whose love has given you
both wealth and life.
Who e'er for honor raised a sword
or for a prize
and now denies it to his Lord,
he is not wise.
For he whom fate shall bless
and grant his tour success
shall have a double claim:
to heaven's grace and worldly fame.

The world deceptively has smiled,
has beckoned me,
and I pursued her, as a child,
so foolishly.
I followed her with eager feet,
the wanton fair;
where none has found a safe retreat,
I hastened there.
Now save me, Jesus Christ,
from that which would entice,
from him who would ensnare,
through this your sign which now I bear.

Since death has torn away from me
my patron lord,
the world, however fair it be,
brings no reward.
So few of all my joys remain:

he took the rest,
to labor for the spirit's gain
is now the best.
And may he share the grace
I strive for in his place,
I grant him half, and more,
and pray we meet at heaven's door.

THE WIFE WHO SENDS HER CHERISHED LORD

(Swelch vrowe sendet lieben man)

The wife who sends her cherished lord
with cheerful heart upon this quest
shall purchase half of his reward,
if she at home but do her best
that all her virtue may declare.
She here shall pray to God for both
and he for both shall battle there.

Wolfram von Eschenbach was born about the year 1170 in
northeastern Bavaria, perhaps at the town of Eschenbach. His
family belonged to the minor nobility and were administrators
of the estates of the Counts of Öttingen, but he was probably a
younger son with no property, income, or position. Wolfram
did have a home of his own, however, a wife whom he dearly
loved, and children. Nevertheless, he moved rather frequently,
perhaps as he changed patrons. Most of the time from 1203 on
he stayed at the boisterous court of Count Hermann of Thurin-
gia, where he doubtless met Walther von der Vogelweide, as
well as many other prominent minnesingers of the day, for
Count Hermann was renowned as a patron of singers. Wolfram
died at some time between 1217 and 1220. Although he is
mentioned in no official document, we know a great deal about
his life because of the highly personal manner in which he reacts
to incidents in the lives of his heroes and because of the close
relationship which he establishes between himself and his lis-

teners. Often Wolfram interrupts the course of a narrative in order to refer to himself and his activities. In one place he claims to be illiterate, which is doubtless a humorous exaggeration. However, it does appear that he did not know Latin and that his knowledge of French was rather elementary. But he did know the German literature of his time well: he valued Hartmann's work, although he did not take the latter's strict conception of chivalric manners very seriously; he was an open adversary of Gottfried von Strassburg who, in his *Tristan and Isolde*, had criticized Wolfram's obscure language; he thought little of Reinmar and the latter's rather unmanly, exaggerated devotion to his aging ladylove; he praised Walther and may even have been on personal, friendly terms with him.

Today Wolfram is known primarily for his courtly epics: *Titurel, Willehalm*, and the great masterpiece of the Middle Ages, *Parzival*. He was the most profound and versatile poet of his time, but his peculiar, acrid humor, his play with strange pictures and symbols, his startling metaphors, and his abruptness of expression made for the difficult style which Gottfried condemned. The other contemporaries who mention him, however, do so with admiration. In his own day Wolfram was famous as a minnesinger as well as for his courtly epics. Of his songs only eight survived. He composed three rather conventional minnesongs, but it is easy to see that he, with his practical common sense, could not get enthusiastic about the traditional plaint of the lover who serves the grand lady whom he must constantly worship in vain. Wolfram states frankly that marriage is much to be preferred to such a frustrating relationship. His five dawn songs, however, are much more natural and fresh. He likes to describe the beginning of day and the awakening of nature, to which he gives a spirit of its own. He experiences the mood of the dawn, and the spring, and the birds which sing for the lovers —nature shows itself to him in its most splendid and sympathetic manifestations. In his dawn songs Wolfram sings of the passion and sorrow of parting and the last happiness before separation with a power, an ingenuity of expression, and a naturalness which break all bonds of convention. Without emphasizing the immorality of the dawn song he shows a strong and healthy joy in the senses. He was an innovator in this type of song in that he gave the watchman a more important role in the drama, for his songs are essentially dramatic. Although Wolfram's verse has more earthy vigor and less conventional manners than that of the other courtly singers of his day, he was always a nobleman, who saw the world only with the eyes of a knight. Neither the *Spielmann* nor the goliard contributed significantly to his art.

The first of the songs below is a dialogue, not between two lovers as in most dawn songs, but between a lady and a watchman. The opening lines present the most striking metaphor in medieval lyric verse. The following poem could be called an 'anti-dawnsong' in that it contrasts the fears and troubles of secret love with the peaceful bliss of the marital relationship. The words are spoken by a man to the watchman. The third poem is a rather traditional May song, perhaps intended to accompany dancing. In the first stanza the singer compares himself favorably with the birds, for the latter sing only through half of the summer and he sings even when the frost (unrewarded love) chills him. He is the nightingale of the second stanza who, although he did not sleep in the winter as did the other birds, is still awake in the spring and is pouring forth his music.

The last two selections are not from Wolfram's minnesongs, but are excerpts from his Arthurian epic, *Titurel*. In both selections the heroine, Sigune, sings of her absent loved one, Schionatulander. The first excerpt shows the verse form as Wolfram composed it, the second is from *The Younger Titurel*, a later version of his work, and reveals how anonymous singers modernized the old Germanic long line by adding interior rhyme. The melody of *The Younger Titurel* is extant and may be that which Wolfram composed.

DAWN STRIKES ITS CLAWS

(Sine klâwen)

'Dawn strikes its claws
through massive clouds and mounts in flight.
It rises with relentless power

94

and with it draws
the graying shadows of the night.
I see the day, which at this hour
will steal the pleasure of the man
whom I admitted fearfully.
I'll get him out now, if I can:
his stately bearing must have blinded me.'

'The song you sing,
O watchman, takes my joy away
and makes more grievous my lament.
The news you bring
each morning at the break of day
gives only sorrow and discontent.
Such words I do not care to hear,
so hold your tongue and let us be,
and I'll reward you, never fear,
if my dear love remains a while with me.'

'He still must go,
sweet lady, say goodbye, that he
may leave as promptly as he came,
and later show
his love for you more stealthily,
preserve his life and his good name.
He trusted in my faithfulness
to get him safely forth from here;
the night has passed when your caress
and kisses bought my aid to bring him near.'

'Sing what you will,
O watchman, sing, but let him stay,
who brought his love and here found mine.
Your rough words fill
us always with intense dismay.
Before the morning star can shine
upon this knight who visits me,
while still no rays of sunlight part

the night, you make him rise and flee
from my bare arms, but never from my heart.'

But still the clear
bright rays the sun cast overhead
and the warning watchman's rude request
caused her to fear
for the gallant knight who shared her bed:
she pressed him closely to her breast.
And yet the knight was strong and brave,
despite the watchman's song above;
their warm and tender parting gave
them kisses (and much more) as spoils of love.

YOUR WONTED SAD REFRAIN

(Der helden minne ir clage)

Your wonted sad refrain
of secret love and pain,
of sours that follow sweets
for him whom woman greets
only at night,
who then must part by day —
that pain and all you say
about it's right.
But silence, watchman, prudent counsel:
I need no more take flight.

For one who can like me
with his beloved be
concealed not from the world,
he'll not be rudely hurled
from love to strife,
nor at the break of day
have need to run away
to save his life,
but can at leisure still embrace
his own sweet generous wife.

(Ursprinc bluomen, loup ûz dringen)

Flowers blossom, buds awaken,
in the air of May the birds sing sweetly in accord;
I, by inspiration taken,
though the frost remain, dear lady, sing without reward.
The wood-singer's merry song
is heard no more the second half of summer long.

Flowers that shine and glisten gaily
shall be studded brighter still with gems of morning dew.
Birds— the brightest, best— do daily
in the nest their children rock and lull the Maytime through.
Then slept not the nightingale;
I'm still awake and sing on mountain and in vale.

Grace from you my song imploring—
for your help is to my song as requisite as breath—
this reward my strength restoring,
I shall sing to you, dear lady, even unto death.
To grant me do not disdain
the consolation which will soothe my long years' pain.

Lady, will my service flourish?
If you grant the favor I desire today it will,
scattering the fears I nourish
and achieving all the youthful dreams I cherish still.
I'm forced now, for short or long,
as you would have, to sing to you your beauty's song.

Noble Lady, your sweet merit
and your charming anger have despoiled me of delight.
Will you heal my wounded spirit,
for a gentle word from you would all my pain requite?
Oh end now my sad lament
by granting that, in this life even, I may be content.

(Ich hân vil âbende   al mîn schouwen)

'Each evening just at dusk   I watch with heart so fond
from window, over street, toward heath and open field beyond,
but all in vain: my lover comes no more.
Thus for a faithless friend   my eyes their bitter tears must
freely pour.

'From window and from rampart   my anxious watch I keep.
To eastward and to west   my longing gaze I sadly sweep
in search of him who long has held my heart;
now younger lovers woo,   and see me not, as one who stands
apart.

'And then to seaward turning,   my eye's full strength employ
to penetrate the distance   in which I think to find my joy,
as though some magic bark distilled of air
might bring me news of him,   and after such long sorrow
banish care.

'So am I then deserted   by happiness so brief?
"Alas," I say, then, for it;   for him alone I'll bear this grief.
For still my heart says he will come again:
one evening he'll appear,   though now he shuns me, driven
by his pain.'

FROM THE YOUNGER TITUREL

(Jamer ist mir entsprungen)

Grief as a river rushes,
pain I cannot still
overwhelms me and crushes
my longing heart upon this pleasant hill.
Comfort, peace, and happiness take flight;
sighs and tears and sorrow
shall I have because of this fair knight.

Since Reinmar der Alte, like Wolfram, does not appear in any official documents, our knowledge of his life is drawn entirely from personal references in his songs and from a few remarks concerning him in the works of his contemporaries. That he was of the minor nobility is indicated by the fact that two manuscripts list him as 'Sir Reinmar,' however, none of the nine manuscripts which contain his works give a place name. Since it is usually assumed that Gottfried had Reinmar in mind when, in *Tristan and Isolde*, he regrets the death of 'the nightingale of Hagenau,' the poet is often called Reinmar von Hagenau. If Reinmar was from Hagenau, he may have been from the place of that name in Austria or from the one in Alsace, or he may have been a member of a von Hagenau family in Strassburg. The language of the manuscripts is not consistent enough to indicate by itself his origin, but most critics favor Alsace as his birthplace. However that may be, it is certain that he spent most of his life in Vienna, probably at the court of the Babenbergs. Indeed, there is no definite evidence that he ever left Vienna, although a line in *Parzival* might indicate that he was at one time a visitor at Count Hermann's court and a vague reference in one of his songs might lead one to believe that he took part in the crusade of 1190-1192. The designation 'the Old' was doubtless given to distinguish him from several more recent Reinmars, for a line in one of Walther's poems seems to say that he died in the prime of life. The most characteristic of his songs—those that are definitely his—must have been written from about 1190 to about 1210, the latter date being approximately that of his death.

In one of his songs Reinmar appears as a rather well-to-do man who holds an important position. Whether or not Reinmar was dependent upon his composition and performance for a living, it is at least certain that he was quite influential on the social mores of Vienna and that he took his duties as an advisor on chivalric manners very seriously. Indeed, this attitude is perhaps most significant to the understanding and appreciation of his verse. In one of his songs he describes himself as an entertainer of courtly society, as one who adds to the joys of the social world. However, he also assumed the duty of educating this society in chivalric ideals. Actually, Reinmar may have been the one who introduced strict courtly manners and conventions into the Viennese court.

When Walther von der Vogelweide was a youth learning the art of minnesong at Vienna, he was strongly influenced by Reinmar, as Walther's early songs clearly show. But the teacher-pupil relationship was soon replaced by a rivalry and a literary feud developed which can be traced in their compositions. Central to the controversy is Reinmar's insistence on the concept of eternal devotion to a lady, who never rewards this devotion or even takes notice of it. To Walther this was carrying the chivalric idealization of the unattainable and unapproachable lady to ridiculous lengths. Although the modern readers, and indeed some of Reinmar's contemporaries, are inclined to agree with Walther, it must be said that Reinmar used this concept very effectively. Reinmar is a reflective poet who is interested in revealing the tragic conflict and contradiction in the idea of *minne*. He controls the moods well and the movement from exaltation to despair as he examines the lover's emotion with sympathetic skill. There is no naiveté and little feeling of direct personal expression, but behind the carefully controlled formalism of his longing there is a heart-felt sadness. If Reinmar uses *minne* as a symbol of all human aspirations, then these are inevitably thwarted and disappointed. He is a virtuoso of courtly lament in its endless, but restricted variations. Joy and sadness are closely related in his songs; indeed the joy often proceeds from an excess of sadness. The lady of whom he sings is distinct, but never described. He is not interested in her, but in the variants of feeling of her suitor—always against a background of specific social manners.

Reinmar is technically skillful. He usually employs a *Stollen* form, always has pure rhyme, and avoids awkward constructions. His language is simple, but highly selective, and shows little evidence of Romance influence. However, though Reinmar composes well-balanced stanzas, there is little continuity between them, often nothing to indicate the order in which they were sung or even whether stanzas having the same form should be considered as making up one or several songs. There is, however, a consistency of mood which gives a certain unity to his songs.

The first of the songs which follow is most typical of Reinmar's verse. In it he bewails the fact that his love is not rewarded, but, unlike other minnesingers, finds the lady quite blameless and beyond reproach. The song is filled with terms of sorrow: 'distress,' 'misery,' 'laments of grief and pain,' 'heart... sore,' 'grievous need,' etc. Yet this sorrow is so manfully borne that 'others think [him] filled with happiness.' In contrast to the dramatic dialogue of Wolfram or the colorful situations of Morungen, only subjective reflection appears. There is no story, nothing happens, and no pictures are described. Reinmar is interested only in the thoughts and feelings of the lover, in the happiness that comes from pain, and the relation of such things to society.

The stanza, 'I Greet You, Woman, Praise Your Name,' is sung less to a single woman than to womankind and is a reminder that faithful service is in itself a moral act and a source of joy. But, nevertheless, the singer cannot repress the wish for a more tangible and direct reward. The lines are a part of his famous song in praise of women which answers Walther's sarcastic attacks on Reinmar's attitude toward *minne*. Walther may not have been convinced, but he was impressed, and he praised the song as an outstanding work of art.

The dirge which begins 'They Say that Summer's with Us Now' is occasional verse, written at the death in 1194 of Duke Leopold v and placed in the mouth of the widow. It is interesting as an example of the use of traditional minnesong structure and language for a marital situation and an actual tragedy.

The stanza, 'A Wondrous Time of Joy Draws Nigh,' is an example of the traditional spring song or Mayday song which greatly antedates the courtly minnesong. Although of folk origin, it was so popular that all of the courtly singers, even including the melancholy Reinmar, composed sometimes in this vein. Quite often such a stanza would serve as a 'nature introduction' to a merry tale, sung between the intervals of dances in the open air.

The last selection given here, though atypical of Reinmar,

is one of his best compositions. Since it is a lady's song and employs a messenger, it goes back to the older tradition of Dietmar. What lends it special charm is the insight into the shy love and sorrow of a woman who almost achieves a real personality. What keeps it from the excellence of Dietmar is its moralizing and insistence on propriety. Reinmar's strong sense of social responsibility will not let him condone the free expression of passion which comes from Dietmar's women. Love must be suffered, not consummated.

NEVER SHOULD A LOVER ASK ADVICE OF ME

(Niemen seneder suoche an mich deheinen rât)

Never should a lover ask advice of me,
for I can't turn aside my own distress.
None has ever suffered greater misery;
yet others think I'm filled with happiness.
Strange it is, I can't complain,
for I can speak no evil of the ladies,
    else you'd hear laments of grief and pain.

Should I say what I have never said before,
oh, this would be disloyalty indeed.
They're the reason why my heart has long been sore
and why I still endure such grievous need.
Better that my heart should break
than that my lips should judge the women harshly:
    I'll be always silent for their sake.

There is nothing that can please them like our prayers,
and yet it gives them pleasure to say, 'No.'
How peculiar are the humors and the airs
which, hidden in their bosoms, grow and grow.
Who would like to win their smile
must stay with them and praise them well.
    That I have done—it helped me only for a while.

Yet the guilt I bear is really not as great
as lack of any recompense has been.
Empty-handed I bewail my sad estate;
my service passes strangely and unseen.
No one else has suffered so.
When I've recovered from these pangs of love
    I'll feel no more of happiness or woe.

I am just a fool to be complaining still
and to pretend that she's at all to blame.
Since I have her in my heart without her will,
how can she help it if my heart's aflame?
Maybe she's unhappy too.
But I must simply leave that as it is;
    I only have my faithfulness to rue.

I GREET YOU, WOMAN, PRAISE YOUR NAME

(Sô wol dir, wîp, wie reine ein nam)

I greet you, woman, praise your name;
how pleasant to the ear, how sweet it is to say!
It would not so deserve its fame,
had you not made it good and kind, as is your way.
One ought to sing your praise in full, but no one can.
Whoever serves you faithfully, he is a joyous man
and one whom life will bless.
You make the whole world light at heart, why can't
    you give me, too, a little happiness?

THEY SAY THAT SUMMER'S WITH US NOW

('Si jehent, der sumer der sî hie)

'They say that summer's with us now,
that all its joys awaken,
and that I'll be happy as before.
Oh, could you only tell me how,

103

for death from me has taken
that which I'll lament forever more.
What good to me is all this cheer and mirth,
since Leopold, the lord of joy, is lying in the earth,
whom I have never known to mourn?
In losing him there was a loss
such as the world has had before in no man ever born.

'Poor soul, how merry I was then
whene'er I thought of him
and how with his my happiness was bound.
That I'll not have such bliss again
makes all the joys grow dim
that I perhaps in life might still have found.
For I have lost the mirror of delight
which I had hoped would make the summer pleasing to my
sight;
but that, alas, has gone for nought.
When I was told that he was dead
the blood welled forth from out my heart and covered every
thought.

'The death of my beloved lord
denies me happiness
and from now on I'll seek for it in vain.
I'll only have as my reward
the struggle with distress
which fills my aching heart with such a pain
that I cannot withhold the bitter tears.
No one but he could make my life worth living through the years,
who now is gone. What's here for me?
Grant him Thy mercy, Lord and God,
for never has a guest with greater virtue come to Thee.'

(Ze fröiden nâhet alle tage)

A wondrous time of joy draws nigh
the waiting world each passing day
to soothe the grief and still the sigh
that hateful winter brings our way.
When barren fields before me lie
my heart is filled with deep dismay.
In wooded vale
my spirits fail,
but soon will sing the nightingale
that spring is victor in the fray.

MESSENGER, HEAR WHAT I SAY

(Lieber bote, nu wirp alsô)

Messenger, hear what I say,
seek him out and tell him this:
if he's well and feeling gay,
then I, too, find naught amiss.
Warn him also, for my sake
to be careful. What might part us
he should never undertake.

If he asks, you should admit
that I'm always well and merry;
if you can, get him to quit
plaints which are not necessary.
For I love him from my heart
and would rather see him than
the day—but do not tell that part.

Ere you let my sweetheart know
that his lady loves him dearly,
first find out how matters go
and hear what I tell you clearly:

if he's faithful to his vow,
tell him what will give him joy
   and my honor will allow.

Should he say he'll soon appear,
I'd be always in your debt;
what he said the last time here
you must tell him to forget
ere he comes again to me.
Why give ear to his request
   when such a thing may never be?

It is death and will not fail
to bring to many grief and dread.
It can make a woman pale
and it often makes them red.
Men may call it love, but they
should call it not-love; woe to him
   who first led woman thus astray.

That I spoke of this so much
shows how great is my despair.
I have not been used to such
nor to sorrows that I bear
and must suffer all unknown.
You must never tell him this;
   it was said for you alone.

7

WALTHER VON DER VOGELWEIDE

The songs of Hartmann, Wolfram, and Reinmar were essentially an aristocratic development of the Provençal troubador compositions and had little in common with the non-courtly songs of Germany. In the works of Walther von der Vogelweide, however, can be seen the influence of the hymns of the monasteries; the didactic and riddle verse of the *Spielleute*; the comic, erotic, and polemic songs of the goliards; as well as the chivalric traditions of *minne*. He was familiar with all of the themes and poetic conventions of his times — religious, popular, and courtly — and employed them in his works with a freshness of language and a metrical proficiency unsurpassed in the history of the medieval lyric.

Although only one official document mentions Walther, a considerable amount of information concerning his life can be gleaned from his works. It is believed that he was born in the southern Tyrol about 1170 of noble, but obscure parents. He learned the art of poetic and musical composition at the court in Vienna where he probably remained until 1198 at which time he began a life of wandering from court to court and patron to patron, which did not end until 1220 when he received a fief from the Emperor Friedrich II. He died about ten years later and is said to be buried in the cathedral at Würzburg. He was famous among the singers of his day and is mentioned in many of their works.

About 80 love songs and 100 *Sprüche* by Walther are extant in a large number of manuscripts. Although he composed some minnesongs in the strictly chivalric tradition, he is better known for love songs of a more personal and natural character in which the forms, but not the spirit of the courtly song appear. In most of his erotic verse a sympathetic, light-hearted, and humorous tone prevails. Walther's chief contribution to Middle High German poetry, however, was not in the genre of the love song, but in that of the *Spruch*. In his *Sprüche*, didactic and political verse was raised to a high and sophisticated level of literature and with them he became an influential social critic of his period and an able propagandist for a strong empire. He supported those who gave leadership and unity to the empire and attacked those, including the pope, who would weaken it. Walther was also a champion of good manners and his later works frequently lament the decline of chivalric idealism and the lack of good taste, as well as the breakdown of law and order. They also betray an increasing concern with his personal religious situation.

Two of the earliest of Walther's songs are 'Now Has the Winter Brought Harm to Us All' and 'Blissfully He Lay.' The dactylic rhythm and the repeated rhyme of the former are the result of the strong influence of Romance song before Walther had developed a style of his own. It is thought to have been composed to a Provençal melody. 'Blissfully He Lay' is the only dawn song which he composed. Considering the general popularity of the type, this fact is at first somewhat surprising. However, when one considers that the dawn song had become quite standardized and inflexible in form before Walther began to compose, one can understand why an imaginative artist would avoid it. Its tragic tone, too, was not in keeping with the poet's usually happy treatment of love. In this song Walther adds nothing new to the conventional dawn song. He does, however, make it more animated by presenting the plaints of both lovers in each stanza, rather than in alternating stanzas.

(Uns hat der winter geschat über al)

Now has the winter brought harm to us all,
meadow and forest are both in his thrall,
where many voices still sang in the fall.
If I were watching the maidens play ball,
soon I'd be hearing the forest birds call.

Could I but slumber the whole winter long!
When I'm not sleeping he does me much wrong,
great is his might and his malice is strong,
yet is he conquered when May sings its song.
Where frost now glistens shall flowers then throng.

BLISSFULLY HE LAY

(Friuntlichen lac)

Blissfully he lay,
the lusty cavalier,
upon a lady's arm.   He saw the morning light
as, gleaming from a distance,   through the mist it broke.
With grief the lady spoke,
'I wish you woe, O Day,
for I can stay no longer   with my handsome knight.
What's known as love is only   a longing and a fear.'

'Lady, I implore
you not to sorrow so.
It's better for us both   that I should now depart,
I see the silver gleam   of the morning star above.'
'O stay with me, my love,
and let us speak no more
of leaving, that you may   not so distress my heart.
Indeed, it is not right.   Why need you haste to go?'

'Lady, it shall be,
I'll stay a while with you.
Now tell me what you wish,   but still it must be brief,
that we may now deceive   the watchers once again.'
'My heart is filled with pain.
Before I shall be free
to lie with you once more   I'll have so much of grief.
Don't stay away too long!   Such nights are all too few.'

'I'll come whene'er I may,
so do not be forlorn.
Though I must now depart   and leave you for a while,
my heart shall still remain   and shall not stir from here.'
'Obey me now, my dear;
you will not stay away
if you are true to me   without deceit or guile.
Alas, the night is gone.   I see the breaking morn.'

'Lady, I must fly!
Permit me now to ride
away from here, to save   your name must I take leave.
So loud and near the watchman   sings his morning song.'
'He will be here ere long,
so we must say goodbye,
but how this sad departure   causes me to grieve!
May God in heaven be   your guardian and your guide!'

The lover soon was gone,
and all his joy had flown.
He left the pretty lady   weeping bitter tears.
But he was always loyal   because he shared her bed.
'Whene'er I hear,' she said,
a melody at dawn,
my heart shall always be   distressed with pain and fears.
A sad and longing woman   I lie here now alone.'

The most delightful of Walther's love songs, 'Under the Linden,'
is not in the courtly tradition and is not about a noble lady but

tells the experience of a simple peasant girl. A comparison between it and 'I Was a Child and Fair to See,' will reveal Walther's knowledge of this or similar goliard songs at the same time that it points up his sympathetic understanding, light humor, and delicate treatment of an episode which the anonymous goliard portrayed in a rather coarse and ribald manner. Although Walther often sang of courtly love, he once declared that 'woman' was a more complimentary term than 'lady', that femininity was preferable to lofty pride. And the naively charming peasant girl who here describes a meeting with her lover well supports his claim.

In the song, 'How Beautiful Her Form and Face,' Walther plays a joke on his listeners. The song follows almost to the end the standard pattern for a particular type of minnesong in which all of the beauties and virtues of the lady are enumerated (a device probably borrowed from several of the Songs of Solomon) and at the end the complaint is made that the lady does not reward her admirer for his many services. Walther, however, at the last minute substitutes a peeping Tom for the forlorn lover with very gratifying results.

UNDER THE LINDEN

(Under der linden)

Under the Linden
I and my lover
softly were bedded in grass and shade.
And if you should wander
there, you'll discover
many a broken bloom and blade.
By the forest, in the dale,
'tandaradei!'
sweetly sang the nightingale.

I went to our meeting
and did not tarry,
for he I loved had gone before.

III

Oh, what a greeting!
Holy Mary,
I'll be blessed for evermore!
Did he kiss me? Yes, and how!
'Tandaradei.'
See how red my lips are now.

My lover had laid
with care meanwhile
a lovely bed of flowers for me.
The village maid
will slyly smile
who walks there past the linden tree
and sees the spot where on that day
'tandaradei'
my head among the roses lay.

If anyone guesses
that we were together
(May God forbid!), I'd surely die.
Of his caresses,
hid by the heather,
may no one know but he and I
and the bird that sang so well:
'tandaradei.'
I can trust it not to tell.

HOW BEAUTIFUL HER FORM AND FACE

(Si wunderwol gemachet wîp)

How beautiful her form and face,
may she give thanks to me ere long,
for both of them I now shall place
with loving care within my song.
I serve the ladies, one and all,
but I have chosen her alone.
To other men may others fall,

I care not how they praise their own,
though they use song and air
that I composed; as I praise here,
            may they praise there.

Her head is so exceeding fair
as only heaven e'er may be,
with it can nothing else compare
in splendor truly heavenly.
Two stars are there and gleaming clear,
I'd like to see myself therein,
would she but hold those stars so near
then might a miracle begin
to make me young once more
and fill with joy the one whose heart
            with love is sore.

God made her cheeks a true delight
in which his richest color glows,
the deepest red, the purest white,
here, like a lily, there, a rose.
I hope it's not a sin to say
I'd rather watch her blushes than
admire the starry Milky Way,
but why should I, O foolish man,
place her so high above me?
My praise would cause me pain, were
            she too proud to love me.

Such lips she has, so full and red,
if I could bring them close to mine
I would arise as from the dead
and nevermore would faint or pine.
Whose cheek she touches with those lips
would gladly have them stay for hours,
for from them such a fragrance drips
as balsam or perfume of flowers.
If she would lend a kiss

I'd give it back whene'er she wished,
        be sure of this.

Her throat, her hands, her feet I've seen
and found how greatly all excelled,
and should I praise what lies between,
I'd but relate what I beheld.
I must confess, no warning cry
was uttered when I saw her bare.
She saw me not when she let fly
the Cupid's dart which still I wear.
I praise the blissful state
in which the lovely woman left her
        bath of late.

Although Walther could compose non-courtly lovesongs and could use the conventional minnesong for humorous purposes, he accepted the chivalric concept of faithful service to a high-born lady and most of his lovesongs follow the general courtly tradition. Even here, however, Walther's sense of humor and his inability to play convincingly the role of a grief-stricken lover lend a very distinctive mood to his verse. Chivalric poetry in general presents love not merely as a highly idealized emotion, but also as a powerful, capricious, often destructive force, against which the individual struggles in vain. The classic example of such a presentation is found in Gottfried's *Tristan and Isolde*. In 'Who Made You, Love, So Fierce and Bold' Walther acknowledges this fatal power of love, but is happy that he is chained to one who meets his complete approval. The song 'When From the Grass the Meadow Flowers Spring' is also a happy one, but it belongs to a type of minnesong, the spring song or May-day song, which was customarily light-hearted. This is a dance song and was doubtless performed to accompany dancing in the open air, perhaps as a part of a spring festival. The personification of May greatly antedates Walther and probably goes back to his pagan ancestors and their worship of various phenomena of nature.

WHO MADE YOU, LOVE, SO FIERCE AND BOLD

(Wer gab dir, minne, den gewalt)

Who made you, love, so fierce and bold;
who gave you power so immense
that you should conquer young and old,
and wisdom offers no defense?
Well, I'll thank God because, at last,
your chains (which I have known so well) now bind me fast
to one whom I adore and praise.
I'll never more be free, so grant me, queen, this favor,
that I may serve you all my days.

WHEN FROM THE GRASS THE MEADOW FLOWERS SPRING

(Sô die bluomen ûz dem grase dringent)

When from the grass the meadow flowers spring
and turn their laughing faces toward the sun
upon a May-day in the morning dew,
and all the birds of field and forest sing
their sweetest songs—for who would be outdone,
what shall I then compare such rapture to?
To half the joys of Paradise.
And yet, if you should ask what can entice
me more than this, I should avow
what pleased my sight most in the past,
and still would, if I saw it now.

For when a lovely and a noble lady,
attired in finest clothes and with her hair
done up in stately manner, walks with friends
of courtly bearing in a garden shady,
and looks about at times with such an air
as might become the sun as it ascends
among the stars, then May can bring

us all its wealth and beauty, yet what thing
shall with this lovely form compare?
We leave May's flowers where they stand
and gaze upon the lady fair.

If you would know the truth, then take my arm
and let us join the festival of May
that now is here with all its joyful treasure.
Look well! Then look upon the ladies' charm
and tell me who will bear the prize away,
and say which wonder gives you greater pleasure.
I know, if I were forced to choose
the one to keep, the other one to lose,
I'd make my choice with no ado.
Sir May, you would be March before
I'd sacrifice my love for you.

In Walther's day there was an empire which consisted largely,
but not exclusively, of German-speaking lands which, however,
were practically autonomous and by no means made up a Ger-
man nation. All of Walther's political verse was directed toward
the establishment of a nation such as France, for example,
represented. It is, therefore, not surprising that he should be
the author of the first patriotic song of German literature. The
line 'eastward here as far as Hungary' indicates that the verses
were composed on the occasion of Walther's return after a long
absence to the Viennese court where he had spent his youth.
Once more a fine sense of humor is apparent, which is as suitable
to his patriotism as to his love.

WELCOME AND WITH ALL GOOD CHEER

(Ir sult sprechen: 'willekomen')

Welcome and with all good cheer
him who brings you stories; I am he.

116

All the other tales told here
were an empty wind. Now come hear me.
First give me my reward,
if it satisfies,
things I'll tell, perhaps, to open wide your eyes.
See what gifts you can afford!

German ladies shall embrace
news of such a nature that they may
better charm us with their grace.
That I'll do for no excessive pay.
What shall be the fee?
I can't reach so high;
I'll be modest if the ladies be not shy,
and will greet me tenderly.

I have travelled far and wide,
have traversed the best of lands indeed;
may misfortune by my guide,
should I make my erring heart concede
that it was impressed
by their foreign ways.
Well, what would I gain by false and empty praise?
German manners are the best!

From the Elbe to the Rhine,
eastward here as far as Hungary,
there the fairest beauties shine
that this wanderer ever hopes to see.
He who understands
lovely forms as well
as I, would swear, by God, our peasant girls excel
fine ladies in all other lands.

German men are all refined,
angels can't surpass the women here;
who thinks otherwise is blind,
so, at least to me, it would appear.

He who seeks in vain
culture, love, and light,
should come into a land where all of these unite.
May I evermore remain!

Although Walther could praise in all good conscience German ladies and German manners, he was usually quite critical of German politics and all of the centrifugal forces which operated against German unity. When the German emperor Heinrich VI died in 1197, the political situation in the Empire became critical. Heinrich's son, Friedrich II, was elected emperor, but Pope Innocent III refused to recognize him, and other candidates for the throne appeared. Walther supported Philip of Swabia, who was crowned in 1198. This is the background for the *Spruch* 'I Heard a River Flow.' The 'wretched kings' mentioned in the poem are the kings of England, France, and Denmark, whom Walther accuses of attempting to gain control of the Empire.

'I Sat upon a Stone,' which is composed in the same *Ton* as 'I Heard a River Flow,' deplores the breakdown of law and order as a result of the imperial interregnum. The absence of peace and justice make impossible the fulfillment of a knight's chief desire, the achieving of wealth, fame, and God's grace. Walther's self-description in the opening lines inspired the well-known painting of him which appears in the Manesse manuscript.

A third political *Spruch*, 'The Cooks Who Serve Our Host,' is a satirical attack on one of the divisive forces. As perhaps the keenest political analyst of his day, he saw great danger to German unity in the increasing number of the semi-autonomous states which were springing up as a result of imperial grants. In the poem he tells the cooks (the advisors and officials of the emperor) to cut off even thicker slices of the Empire for the princes. He then reminds them of the fate of the Byzantine emperor whose country was divided up by the leaders of the crusaders and who was finally deposed.

I HEARD A RIVER FLOW

(Ich horte ein wazzer diezen)

I heard a river flow,
saw bright fish come and go.
I saw the world: all things concealed
in reed and grass, in wood and field
that creep or walk or fly
between the earth and sky.
I saw all this and can relate
that all things live in fearful hate,
that beast and reptile corps
wage unrelenting wars
and birds with their own kind unite
to carry on a ceaseless fight.
But this I also saw —
the beasts have still their law.
They have their kings and rights
and choose their lords and knights.
But Oh, you German lands
where no one voice commands,
how can the flies their monarch know
and German honor fall so low!
Unite as oft of old!
The foreign crowns grow bold,
and wretched kings reveal their greed.
Lord Philipp, wear the diadem
and bid us follow where you lead!

I SAT UPON A STONE

(Ich saz ûf eime steine)

I sat upon a stone,
leg over leg was thrown,
upon my knee an elbow rested
and in my open hand was nested

my chin and half my cheek.
My thoughts were dark and bleak:
I wondered how a man should live,
to this no answer could I give.
Could man three things enjoy
and none the rest destroy?
The two are worldly wealth and fame,
which often bring each other shame;
the third is Heaven's grace,
which takes the highest place.
I wish that I might have all three,
but it, alas, can never be
that one man's heart should hold
both worldly fame and gold
and aught of Heaven's favor, too.
No road will let them through
where treason would betray you
and naked force would slay you.
Peace and right are wounded sore;
the three have no protection till
the two are well and strong once more.

THE COOKS WHO SERVE OUR HOST

(Wir suln den kochen râten)

The cooks who serve our host
and carefully dispense his store
their fears should overcome
and cut the princes' roast
a little larger than before
and thicker by a thumb.
A tasty roast was carved in Greece
with vulgar manners and caprice,
they should have left it in one piece,
the roast was sliced too thin.
The princes forced their host to go
and chose another one for show.

Who loses his possessions so
were better off were he no roast to win.

Walther used the *Spruch* for political and didactic purposes, but
he employed it also, like the minnesong, purely for entertain-
ment. An effective source of humor then as now was the telling
of incidents that happened to the narrator which place him in
a less than heroic position. Such a song is 'Sir Gerhart Atze
Shot My Horse.' Since there are records of a Gerhart Atze at
the Thuringian court and since Walther in another poem refers
to him and the loss of his horse, it is possible that the incident
related here actually occurred. Even though the song is (or
pretends to be) bitter, its humor appears when Walther asks
someone to hold his staff so that he can make an oath with both
hands raised. The 'mutual lord' was, of course, Count Hermann.

SIR GERHART ATZE SHOT MY HORSE

(Mir hat her Gerhart Atze ein pfert)

Sir Gerhart Atze shot my horse
at Eisenache dead.
My grievances I now shall lay
before our mutual lord.
The beast was worth a lot, of course,
but just hear what he said
when it appeared he'd have to pay
the debt that he'd ignored.
He speaks of pain and need
and says my horse indeed
was brother to the steed
which bit his thumb in half
and caused him grief thereby.
I swear with both hands high
all that is just a lie.
Who here will hold my staff?

121

Walther's religious verse belongs to that which is generally believed to have been written in his later years. It is characterized by sincerity of mood and simplicity of expression. The best known of these songs is his crusade hymn, 'Now My Life Has Gained Some Meaning.' There are various theories about the time of origin: one scholar maintains that it was written to support the crusade of Friedrich I, in 1189; another that it was written, perhaps in Jerusalem, when Walther was taking part in the crusade of 1219-21; a third believes that it was composed while Walther, as an old man, was on the crusade of 1228. However this may be, it was certainly written as a hymn to be sung by pilgrims and crusaders. One cannot say that Walther was particularly successful as a hymn writer; however, the work is important for the fact that its music is the oldest extant by a minnesinger.

A part, but not all of the music for the religious *Spruch*, 'Thou Most Exalted God, How Rare My Praise to Thee,' is also extant. The work is appealing in its humility and frank confession of the singer's human weakness when he sorrowfully but honestly acknowledges his inability to practice doctrinal Christian love. His more characteristic optimism appears in the last song, a prayer for guidance and grace. The *Ton* in which this *Spruch* was composed was Walther's favorite and he used it for a total of fifteen different poems. It was called by the sixteenth century mastersingers the *Friedrichston* and may actually have been composed by Walther in honor of Duke Friedrich of Austria, who died in Palestine in 1198.

NOW MY LIFE HAS GAINED SOME MEANING

(Nû alrest leb' ich mir werde)

Now my life has gained some meaning
since these sinful eyes behold
the sacred land with meadows greening
whose renown is often told.
This was granted me from God:
to see the land, the holy sod,
which in human form He trod.

Splendid lands of wealth and power,
I've seen many, far and near,
yet of all are you the flower.
What a wonder happened here!
That a maid a child should bear,
Lord of all the angels fair,
was not this a wonder rare?

Here was He baptized, the Holy,
that all people might be pure.
Here He died, betrayed and lowly,
that our bonds should not endure.
Else our fate had been severe.
Hail, O cross, thorns and spear!
Heathens, woe! Your rage is clear.

Then to hell the Son descended
from the grave in which He lay,
by the Father still attended,
and the Spirit whom none may
give a name: in one are three,
an arrowshaft in unity.
This did Abraham once see.

When He there defeated Satan,
ne'er has kaiser battled so,
He returned, our ways to straighten.
Then the Jews had fear and woe:
watch and stone were both in vain,
He appeared in life again,
whom their hands had struck and slain.

To this land, so He has spoken,
shall a fearful judgment come.
Widows' bonds shall then be broken
and the orphans' foe be dumb,
and the poor no longer cower
under sad misuse of power.
Woe to sinners in that hour!

Christians, heathen, Jews, contending,
claim it as a legacy.
May God judge with grace unending
through his blessed Trinity.
Strife is heard on every hand:
ours the only just demand,
He will have us rule the land.

THOU MOST EXALTED GOD, HOW RARE MY PRAISE TO THEE

(Vil wol gelobter got, wie selten ich dich prîse)

Thou most exalted God, how rare my praise to Thee,
although Thou givest both my song and melody!
How could I so neglect to honor Thy decree?
My works are not the best, nor do I show true love
to Thee, my gracious Lord, nor to my Christian brother.
I always cared more for myself than for another.
Oh Father, Son, Thy spirit guide me from above!
How may I love the one who causes me to smart?
I must prefer the man who always takes my part.
Forgive my other sins, I cannot change my heart.

WITH JOY MAY I ARISE TODAY

(Mit saelden müeze ich hiute ûfstân)

With joy may I arise today,
Lord God, and in Thy keeping stay,
although I ride from one land to another.
Lord Christ, let there be seen in me
the power of Thy charity,
and keep me for the sake of Thy dear mother.
An angel guarded her from danger
and Thee, when Thou wert in the manger,
as man so young, as God so old.
With humble service and with firm endeavor

124

among the beasts did Gabriel
watch Mary and her Infant well
and loyally within the fold.
So care for me, and let Thy mercy never
Thy blessed grace from me withhold.

8

NEIDHART VON REUENTHAL

Walther refers disparagingly to Neidhart's uncouth themes and Wolfram mentions his pretentious peasants; otherwise we know no more of Neidhart than can be derived from the occasional personal references in his songs. These tell of a Bavarian knight who had a very modest estate and sang at the court of Duke Ludwig I of Bavaria. He took part in a crusade, either that of 1217-19 or that of 1227-28. About the year 1233 he fell out of favor with the new ruler, Duke Otto II, lost his property, and was obliged to leave Bavaria in order to find a new sponsor. He went to Austria and was granted a small fief by Duke Friedrich II, who was himself a minnesinger. Later he apparently entered the service of the Austrian nobleman Otto von Lengenbach. Neidhart must have been born about 1190 and he died after the year 1236.

The influence of goliard and *Spielmann* songs which is sometimes apparent in the verse of Walther von der Vogelweide is much more obvious in the compositions of Neidhart. Although the latter employs for the most part the sophisticated forms and frequently the chivalric expressions of the traditional minnesong, he uses them to treat peasants and peasant scenes, especially those having to do with indoor and outdoor dances. He thus creates a new type of lyric, which has been called the courtly village song. In lively dance rhythms Neidhart sings of village people and events with the superior, often mocking tones of the nobleman, and spices his colorful reality with burlesque humor. All but one of his songs fall into two groups, the summer songs and the winter songs. The former were perhaps written in the early part of Neidhart's career and, in keeping with the season and the poet's youth, are generally more lighthearted and spirited than the latter. Most of the winter songs were composed while the poet was living in Austria. The two groups of songs differ with regard to structure. Although at first glance it may seem complex, the basic pattern of the summer songs is quite simple and actually represents little more than ingenious variations of the rhymed couplets which the *Spielleute* had been using for generations. The winter songs have the traditional tripartite structure of the minnesong, made up of two *Stollen* and an *Abgesang*, and have metrical and rhyme patterns which are often rather complicated and more characteristic of the courtly song of his day. Both summer and winter songs usually begin with a stanza which describes the season and is followed by stanzas which dramatically relate, often in dialogue form, some village incident. Several of the summer songs consist merely of arguments between a village lass and her mother as to whether the former is to go to the dance. This situation and its treatment is drawn from the Latin *altercatio*, or argumentative song, and was especially popular among the goliard composers. Whatever the incident or situation, however, its narration frequently does not carry over into the last stanza, which deals rather with the poet's own hopes, joys, or sorrows, and often contains his name. In keeping with the accepted summer: joy—winter: sadness symbolism the final stanza of the summer songs shows a happy mood, that of the winter a sorrowful one. In the case of a love song, the narrator's prospects look good in the summer and rather bleak in the winter. Although the narrator takes part in the village activities and even competes with the rude farmers for the favor of rustic maidens, it should not be assumed that these accounts are autobiographical. Neidhart played and sang for dances, it is true, but these were held in the halls or gardens of castles, and the dancers were knights and ladies.

The mixture of chivalric and popular elements in Neidhart's verse often produces incongruous, almost grotesque effects. The ethereal and melancholy longing of the minnesong can change abruptly to the coarse expression of the goliard song; the lovely and remote lady of courtly verse becomes the simple, all-too-human peasant girl; the romantic illusion is destroyed by an almost brutal reality. The impression is frequently one of satire and caricature: the sharp contrasts sometimes make the peasants and the peasant scenes ridiculous; sometimes it is chivalric romanticism which is made to look foolish. Neidhart composed for an audience which knew and was perhaps surfeited with the traditional minnesong, and they would have immediately recognized the incongruity and humor of using courtly expressions and metrics to treat peasants.

Neidhart's songs were very popular in his day and were frequently imitated by composers throughout the entire subsequent history of courtly verse. Nearly six hundred of Neidhart's stanzas are extant and more of his melodies have survived than those of any other secular lyric composer of his century. Five manuscripts have songs attributed to him. Those containing most of the texts believed to be genuine (there are many pseudo-Neidhart songs) date from the fourteenth and fifteenth centuries, the earliest one from about a century after his death.

The first five songs given here are summer songs, composed to be sung at outdoor dances, probably in the court-yard or garden of a castle. Neidhart perhaps sang the first stanza while the dance leaders were going through the first step of the dance, paused while the step was performed by the entire group, sang the second stanza while the leaders demonstrated the second step, etc. These outdoor dances were performed by the company as a whole, whereas the indoor dances were executed in smaller groups of two to four members. Each of the songs begins by welcoming the spring which has brought the young people out into the fields. In 'Such Delightful Meadows' the narrator follows this nature introduction by inviting all of the girls to come out and dance. His invitation is followed by an 'argument' between two girls in which the peasant boys are unfavorably compared with the Knight of Reuenthal. The song 'Barren Were the Meadows and Forsaken' follows a similar pattern except that the narrator does not enter directly into the discussion and that the dispute is between a maid and her mother. The incongruity of the beautiful descriptions of nature and the rather earthy language of the village maiden is particularly striking. The third song, 'Field, Meadow, Forest, as You See,' is distinctive in that the nature theme is carried through the entire song in a consistent development: the beauties of nature lead to the beauty of the young people in their bright spring clothing, which leads in turn to the singer, whose duty it is to teach them to enjoy life. The metrical pattern with its spritely rhythm shows how close Neidhart adheres to the folk tradition: if the last three lines of the stanza are combined there is a simple four-line stanza consisting of two couplets. The reference to the 'vale of tears' in the last strophe is a play on the author's name, Reuenthal, which it translates. The following song, 'The Woods Were Bare and Gray,' begins with a description of nature and an invitation by the singer for the girls to come and dance. Once more the charms of nature are associated with those of the narrator's sweetheart. In this song are no discordant notes: the leafy trees, the meadow flowers, the singing of the birds, the warm rays of the sun, and the dancing village maiden combine to produce a harmonious, idyllic scene. The last of the summer songs is more typical. After describing the beauties of spring, Neidhart presents the contrasting picture of the ugly old peasant woman and her wild, ungainly dancing.

SUCH DELIGHTFUL MEADOWS

(Ine gesach die heide)

Such delightful meadows
I've never seen,
such changing shades and shadows
of forest green.
May reveals itself in wood and heather.
Come, maidens, all together
and dance a merry roundelay to greet the
summer weather.

Praise from many voices
now hails the May,
and field and wood rejoices

in colors gay,
where before were seen no leaves or flowers.
Beneath the linden bowers
a group of youths and pretty maidens dance
                              away the hours.

No one's heart is laden
with grief or care.
Come, each shapely maiden,
so sweet and fair,
deck thyself as Swabians desire thee,
Bavarians admire thee,
with silken ribbons on thy blouse from neck
                              to hips attire thee.

'Why bother?' answered, weeping,
a village maid.
'The stupid men are sleeping,
so I'm afraid.
Honor and delight are but a fable,
the men are all unstable,
to court a woman faithfully and well, they're
                              quite unable.'

'Let's hear no more of sadness,'
thus spoke her friend,
'We'll all grow old with gladness,
for there's no end
of suitors for a maid whose good, and jolly.
Such mournful talk is folly;
I have a lover that can drive away all melancholy.'

'If thou canst show a lover
for whom I'd care,
this belt thy waist shall cover
which now I wear.
Tell his name whom thou art thus commending,
whose love is so unending.

I dreamed of thee last night and learned that
                      thou art just pretending.'

'Everybody knows him
as Reuenthal.
His merry songs disclose him
to one and all.
I like him and repay him for his singing.
For him shall I be springing
about in all my finery. But hark, the bell is
                                    ringing.'

BARREN WERE THE MEADOWS AND FORSAKEN

(Blôzen wir den anger ligen sâhen)

Barren were the meadows and forsaken
until the summer came to warm and waken,
flowers pressed through grass and clover then.
Once again
summer now is opening the roses
and making lovely heath and glen.

Nightingale and thrush, we hear them singing,
with the sound the hills and vales are ringing.
They sing their songs of joyous summertime
as they climb.
May has brought us happiness and beauty:
the heath is blooming in its prime.

Spoke a maid, 'The dew is on the heather,
see the splendor summer brings together.
The trees that in the wintertime were bare
everywhere
wave their leafy branches in the breezes.
The nightingales are singing there.

'Losa, hear the songs of birds resounding,
they greet the May from all the trees surrounding.
I fancy, we are free of winter now.
Wierat, thou
must dance more spritely, wouldst thou gain my favor,
beneath the linden's leafy bough.

'Spring's the time for each to choose a lover,
Roses blossom 'neath the forest's cover
and I shall have a crown of roses red
on my head
when I'm dancing hand in hand so gaily
with such a handsome knight,' she said.

'Daughter, think no more of bold advances.
Should'st thou disturb the nobles at the dances,
who are not the sort for folk as we,
I forsee
thou willst have a lot of pain and trouble.
A sturdy farmer covets thee.'

'Let a heifer wed the worthy farmer!
My hope is for a stately knight in armor.
Why should I take a farmer as my man?
Never can
I be happy with a rustic lover.
A knight alone will suit my plan.'

'Daughter, don't despise his lowly station
to win a stupid noble's admiration.
This has caused your friends distress and pain.
All in vain
are thy promises, I tell thee truly,
thy wilfulness I never could restrain.'

'Mother mine, stop scolding, and believe me,
I would love him though my friends should leave me,
I never hid my wishes, I recall.

One and all
may the people know whom I have chosen,
for he's the knight of Reuenthal.'

FIELD, MEADOW, FOREST, AS YOU SEE

(Heid anger walt in fröden stât)

Field, meadow, forest, as you see,
have festively adorned themselves in all the finery
that May has placed at their command.
Let us sing,
glad with spring:
summer has come into the land.

Come out of your rooms, you pretty maids,
and onto the streets; no bitter wind will chill
                              your promenades,
and ice and snow have gone away.
Come together
to the heather;
birds are singing, once more gay.

They all are now repaid for pain.
But heed what I have said and come and look
                              upon the plain;
and see how summertime can bless,
as a friend,
it will send
every tree a leafy dress.

But those of you who can aspire
to something better, now put on your holiday attire
and show us what your silver buys.
We shall see,
gay and free,
many flowers before our eyes.

133

Though I possess a vale of tears,
this lovely summer sets me free from all my pain
and fears.
And now that winter's rage is spent,
I shall teach
youth to reach
for joy, such is my firm intent.

THE WOODS WERE BARE AND GRAY

(Der walt stuont aller grîse)

The woods were bare and gray,
in ice and snow they lay,
but warmer skies have clothed each bough.
See them now,
maidens fair,
and dance among the flowers there.

From many tiny throats
I heard the silver notes
of little birds in sweetest song.
Flowers throng
in grass and briar,
the meadow dons her spring attire.

I love the charms of May;
I saw my darling play
and dance beneath the linden's crown.
Its leaves bent down,
every one,
to shade her from the radiant sun.

ON THE MOUNTAIN AND IN THE GLEN

(Ûf dem berge und in dem tal)

On the mountain and in the glen
swells the music of bird's again.

Now are seen
fields in green.
Away with you, Winter, your breath is too keen.

Trees which were standing so long in gray
have all new leaves and among them play
birds of the wood.
This does one good:
they greet the May as warblers should.

A wrinkled old hag who had fought with death
days and nights for life and breath
danced like a sheep
with a bound and a leap
and knocked the younger ones down in a heap.

The three winter songs which are given here are fairly represen-
tative of Neidhart's winter songs in general. Like the summer
songs, they were composed to be sung at dances, but the dancing
was done inside and the dances themselves were of a different
kind. The descriptions are somewhat more realistic than in the
summer songs; the humor is more pronounced, much sharper,
and directed not only at the pretentious and boorish farm boys,
but also at the timid, quite unheroic knight who serves as nar-
rator. It is not entirely coincidence that two of the three songs
consist of seven stanzas, for this was a favorite number with
Neidhart which produced the type of symmetry for which he
strove. The first song, 'Children, Ice is Here, So Ready Up a
Sleigh,' well illustrates his symmetrical treatment of a situation.
The first stanza gives the nature introduction, the next two de-
scribe the preparations for the dance. In the third stanza the
singer makes some personal (and slightly risqué) comments
about women's clothing, the following two stanzas tell of an
amusing, slapstick episode, and the last stanza presents the
singer's lament, in this case about the trials of a property owner.
The peasant Engelmar appears in several of the winter songs as
the rival of the singer. His name, which in various religious

works appears as a synonym for 'God,' is used ironically. Neid-
hart begins the second song, 'Sing, My Golden Cock, I'll Give
Thee Grain,' not with his usual salute to the season but with
the plaint, which in other poems appears at the end. In this case
it is not the winter which inspires the song, but the request of
the singer's sweetheart. The references to dances in the poem
are interesting. The *ridewanz* was apparently danced in groups of
three, each one composed of a man and two women or a woman
and two men. It was a lively dance as compared to the more
stately 'courtly dance' which the villagers performed while they
caught their breath. The 'fiddle' mentioned in the poem is the
medieval German *gîge*, a flat-topped, bowed-stringed instrument
with a pear-shaped body like the later lute. The incongruities
which characterize so much of Neidhart's work are nowhere
more apparent than in the third winter song, 'Winter's Evil
Art.' It begins with the apparent sincerity of a true love song,
but, as it continues, we see a grotesquely amusing hero develop,
a knight who is in love with a peasant girl whom he addresses
as 'lady mine.' He is a most unknightly knight who is bullied
and frightened by his country bumpkin rivals. The final stanza,
however, reverts to the sincere and lyrical mood of the begin-
ning. The next-to-the-last stanza is interesting in that it seems
to be a parody of a stanza in Walther's song, 'Welcome and with
All Good Cheer.' Throughout the song courtly expressions and
conventions are employed only to have the chivalric illusion
destroyed by reference to one or another peasant lout. The
mirror which Engelmar takes is mentioned in several of Neid-
hart's poems and possibly is a symbol borrowed from religious
writings where the devil uses a mirror to entice one to vanity
and worldly actions. One stanza of the original was omitted in
the translation.

CHILDREN, ICE IS HERE, SO READY UP A SLEIGH

(Kind, bereitet iuch der sliten ûf daz îs)

Children, ice is here, so ready up a sleigh
for the dreary winter's cold.

It has stolen from the meadow all its golden treasure,
crowns of lindens, once so green, have turned to gray,
birds have left their forest fold.
All of that has come because we roused the Frost's displeasure.
Only see how he through field and heath did wander!
Now their blooms are drab and pale,
now has flown the nightingale
to distant meadows yonder.

I could use the counsel of a prudent friend
on a matter that is pressing:
where shall all the young folks come for merriment and playing?
Megenwart has quite a spacious room to lend.
If to this you give your blessing,
there we'll gather on the holiday for roundelaying,
for his daughter wants us and it isn't far.
Tell your friends, they must, if able,
see the dance beneath the table
performed by Engelmar.

Get the news to Kunigund, for she will go,
she loves dancing through and through
and has bitterly complained that she is never told.
Gisel, go to Jiutendorf and let them know,
say that Ella must come too.
They have always been my friends, the young ones and the old.
Child, do not forget to speak with Hedwig now
and insist that she be there.
Tell them all, they should not wear
their shawls down to the brow.

As for shawls upon the head, I'll speak my mind
to the women everywhere
who would show their modesty to lovers they possess.
Move them higher up in front and down behind,
so your necks will not be bare.
Shawls do little good when there's no collar on the dress.
Women always have been safe about the head,

it's secure in any case.
What befalls another place
they also need not dread.

Eppe tried to teach some manners all around
(he was aided by his flail),
but the stick of Master Adelbert brought peace once more.
This was started by an egg that Ruprecht found
(or the devil had for sale.)
He would throw it 'cross the room at Eppe, so he swore.
Eppe soon was mad as he was bald and thin;
'Don't you dare,' he grimly said.
Ruprecht hit him on the head
and egg ran down his chin.

Friedelieb with Gotelinde then was seen:
Engelmar with rage was wild.
If it will not bore you, I'll relate the whole affair.
Eberhard, the farmer, had to step between,
they were partly reconciled,
otherwise they'd each have seized the other by the hair.
They, like stupid ganders that had lost their wits,
eyed each other all day long.
He who led the rest in song
was, as always, Fritz.

Once my hair was dressed as fits a cavalier,
brushed and curled in perfect trim.
That is all forgotten in the worries of my fief,
salt and grain I need to buy throughout the year.
How have I offended him
who has burdened stupid me with house and land and grief?
Little were the debts to him, which now I rue,
but my curses aren't so small
when I there at Reuenthal
wonder what to do.

SING, MY GOLDEN COCK, I'LL GIVE THEE GRAIN

(Sinc an, guldîn huon! ich gibe dir weize)

'Sing, my golden cock, I'll give thee grain!'
(at her voice
I rejoice)
spoke the pretty maid for whom I sigh.
Thus a dunce's hopes are raised in vain
seasons through.
Were it true,
no one's spirit then would be so high,
no one else's heart would beat so light.
Will her careless gaiety
ever free
me from all the sorrows of my plight?

Listen! Hear the dancing at the inn!
Every man
go who can,
there the women wait, a merry throng.
Soon we'll see the ridewanz begin.
Tarradiddle
goes the fiddle,
lusty peasant youths break forth in song.
Each in turn sings out his verse with pride,
shakes the room with lungs of brass.
Noblegrass
dances with a maid on either side.

Move out all the chairs and clear the floor;
take the tables
to the stables
and we'll dance till feet and ankles hurt.
Open up the windows and the door;
let the breeze
cool their knees,
blowing through each village wench's skirt.

When the leaders stop to rest a little,
then we'll all, great and small,
short and tall,
step a courtly dance once to the fiddle.

Gozbreht, Willebolt, Gumpreht, and Eppe,
Willebrand,
hired hand,
Werenbolt and also youngster Tutze,
Megenbolt, the farmer's son, and Reppe,
Irenwart,
Sigehart,
Giselher and Frideger and Utze—
he's the stupid oaf from Holingare.
He goes courting every day,
so they say,
but the girls don't like him anywhere.

Never has a bumpkin looked so grand,
nor so flighty;
God Almighty,
how he struts in line before the rest!
More than two hands wide the leather band
of his sword,
like a lord
in his new and gaily-colored vest,
scraps of every shape and hue are there,
fancy shirt, embroidered pants,
see him prance
in a garb no other fool would wear.

His attire is rustic as can be,
it's absurd.
So I've heard,
he's been wooing Engel's daughter, Pearl.
All such hopes are futile, I foresee.
She's a prize
of shape and size

to win the admiration of an earl.
Good advice I'll give him: let him try
someone else; for all his pain
what he'll gain
he can take to Mayence in his eye.

Though his clothes are colorful and gay
and he's dressed
in his best,
he should know she simply can't abide him.
He has hung around her every day;
I became
red with shame
when I saw her sitting down beside him.
If I win this maid who looks so pretty,
I shall give to her my all,
Reuenthal,
for her own: this is my fabled city.

WINTER'S EVIL ART

(Winter, dîniu meil)

Winter's evil art
strips the forest of its leaves
and flowers from the blooming earth.
Summer, joy has vanished from thy merry retinue.
Many a happy heart
now in bitter sadness grieves
which was made for only mirth.
How could a maid whom I before all others would pursue
still appear
not to hear
the serenade with pleasure
which I sang with all the fervor I possess
and yet today preserve and treasure
that she may never find a limit to my faithfulness.

Should my constancy
and devotion through the year
afford me naught but her rejection,
then might I repent, and rightly, this unhappy quest.
It was told to me,
who was always faithful here
would gain in fortune and affection.
With thee to comfort, Lady Luck, my hope is for the best:
that she may mend
and show her friend
less extreme vexation.
Could this be, perhaps the end might still be good.
Grant her evil temper moderation!
Woe, that women never treat their lovers as they should.

For this love of mine
many wish me only ill.
Now hear my plaint with sympathy,
never have I needed wise and prudent counsel more.
Erph and Adelwine
cause me trouble still,
before my time this ages me.
No one can imagine what I've suffered heretofore.
All this year,
so I hear,
they have sought her favor
whom I'll always love and wish to be my own.
Mistress of a heart that ne'er shall waiver,
thou shallst never comfort any man but me alone.

Thou must lock the door
which will close those ears of thine,
that they no jealous words may hear
which might make me seem to thee otherwise than good.
Mark such talk no more,
oh my darling, lady mine,
that is not fitting for thy ear.

Listen to a faithful friend's advice, as each one should.
Kuenebrecht,
Engeknecht,
forward and deceiving,
sue for thy affection, Lady, have them go.
They are why my loving heart is grieving,
they have ever been the source of secret, bitter woe.

Only see my hair,
it is colored like the snow!
Despite my age it makes me gray
that I suffer grief from peasant louts because of her.
There is Engelmare;
he's a reason I am so.
The mirror he still has today
which he once did take from Vriderun, the villager.
From then on
I have gone
courting her no longer.
save with timid steps and timid heart and fear,
and my sorrow waxes ever stronger
that my aching heart desires the maid whom he holds dear.

Westward to the Rhine,
from the Elbe to the Po,
I know the countries all around.
All their borders do not hold so many brazen louts
as a county line
here in Austria, you know.
Many new ones every day are found.
See, there's one who's caused a lot of trouble hereabouts.
Wankelbolt,
he's a dolt,
me he would discredit
(he's a leader there in Lyingdale, it's said),
and the bastard really will regret it.
If he gets too saucy, I'll put holes right through his head.

Love once came to me:
Oh, if Love had but remained!
I came and found the roses fair.
See, I plucked a rose, but soon it lost its loveliness.
Pain and misery
drove away the joy I gained.
I'll tell what I discovered there:
I broke the rose, a wretched thorn then caused me sore distress,
so that I,
though I sigh,
let no roses prick me,
neither look to see what roses I may find.
Many roses raise their thorns to stick me,
but I know there still are roses which are kind.

9

THE TRADITIONAL MINNESONG IN THE THIRTEENTH CENTURY

The general development of the lyric verse composed by aristocratic singers during the thirteenth century was in the direction of an increased complexity of form and a decreased emphasis on chivalric ideals. For the knightly singers deviated more and more from the simple verse structure of the *Spielleute* at the same time that they, following the lead of Walther and Neidhart, came ever closer to them with regard to content. Many dancing songs and dance *Leiche* were composed, the love of knights for village maidens was frequently treated, and even the relationship between knights and ladies sometimes followed the popular rather than the strictly courtly tradition. Especially during the latter half of the century did a deterioration of chivalric concepts take place. This doubtless would have occurred in any case, for the idealism of chivalry was too far removed from reality to last long; however, the weakening of the Empire which followed the end of the Hohenstaufen period brought about a lessening of the importance of the knightly class as well as a general degeneration of law and order, which was not conducive to chivalry.

The changes in the life and culture of the nobility were reflected in the works of many of the composers, but not all of them. For in parts of the German-speaking lands the ideals of chivalry were still a vital component of the culture and even where this was not true there was a reluctance to depart from the ideas, forms, and expressions of the great masters of the preceding century. The songs of Heinrich von Morungen, Reinmar von Hagenau, Hartmann, and Wolfram continued to be popular and many singers saw no reason to experiment with new formulas when the old ones were still well received. Much of this traditional courtly verse is either directly imitative or a rather barren reworking of outworn themes by means of trite expressions and symbols which were no longer meaningful. The best of the traditional minnesongs of the thirteenth century, however, have the freshness and originality of the classical minnesong and witness to the fact that the subjects and conventions of chivalric verse, though limited, could lend themselves to endless new variations.

The first of the thirteenth century composers to be treated here, Heinrich I, Count of Anhalt, was especially conservative in his style. Indeed, the two songs of his which are extant remind one of the period of strong Romance influence and are more similar in form and vocabulary to those of Rudolf von Fenis than to those of any of his contemporaries or immediate predecessors. Heinrich was a son-in-law of Hermann of Thuringia and doubtless learned the art of poetic and musical composition from the many singers who visited the latter's court. He was an important political figure of his day and, like Walther, a staunch supporter of Philipp of Swabia and later of Friedrich II. Heinrich became ruler of Anhalt in 1212, abdicated in 1242, and died ten years later. The motif which appears in the first two lines below was previously used by Bernart de Ventadorn from whom it may have been borrowed.

ASIDE, FOR I MUST FEEL THE BREEZE

(Stâ bi, lâ mich den wint an waejen)

Aside, for I must feel the breeze
that blows from her, the mistress of my heart.
How could it bring perfumes as these,
were it not filled with love in every part.
When my heart was driven forth, it fell into her snare,
and yet, 'God guard her honor,' is my prayer.
Her lovely lips are rosy red; if I could only kiss them once,
I'd ne'er grow old, I swear.

146

I saw the fairest in all the lands
and I can never sing of others now.
To her bright eyes and smooth, white hands,
wherever she may be, I'll always bow.
If with this shapely lady I might breed some children strong,
or just make love to her the whole night long!
Oho! But that would be too much: 't would be enough, if in her
service I might sing my song.

Just as conservative as Heinrich of Anhalt was the minnesinger
whose works appear under the name, The Margrave von Hohen-
burg. Diepold, Margrave of Vohburg, was a member of a noble
family whose ancestral castle was located between Nürnberg
and Regensburg. He was born about 1180 and is first mentioned
in a document of the year 1200. After his marriage to Mathilde,
Countess of Andechs, the widow of Friedrich von Hohenburg,
Diepold appears in various records as Margrave von Hohenburg.
He was a friend of Emperor Friedrich II and spent some time
with him in Italy. He was also apparently on good terms with
Duke Leopold VI of Austria and may have taken part in the
latter's crusade of 1219. Diepold is last mentioned in a docu-
ment of 1223.

Although Diepold was some ten years younger than Walther
von der Vogelweide and was composing at the same time as
Neidhart von Reuenthal, there is no indication in his songs that
he was familiar with the works of either. His occasional use of
dactyls and repeated rhyme relate, as do those of Heinrich, to the
earlier period when Provençal influences were stronger, and
remind one especially of Friedrich von Hausen. Six minnesongs
by Diepold have been preserved. Their tone and content is
purely chivalric; there is no humor, satire, parody, or noncourtly
love. With the exception of the one dawn song, they are pri-
marily devoted to praising the charms and virtues of the object
of the narrator's love. The mood is cheerful and only a single
song can be called a plaint. Diepold's language is refreshingly
simple and his thoughts and feelings are expressed directly with
no poetic adornment. His *Töne* also are simple; all begin with

four lines rhyming *a b a b*, which in two songs is followed by
c d c d, in a third by two couplets, in a fourth by *a b a b*, and in a
fifth by *b b b*. Only the dawn song has a rhyme scheme which
is even moderately complex. With regard to content this song
is quite traditional. Its only unusual feature is the strong sense
of duty which causes the watchman to identify his fate with that
of the lovers, as is indicated when he speaks of 'us' and 'we.'

I WATCH TO GUARD A NOBLE'S LIFE

(Ich wache um eines ritters lîp)

'I watch to guard a noble's life
and save your honor, lovely wife:
wake him, lady!
God grant this favor to us three,
that no one may awake but he:
wake him, lady!
It's time to go,   and don't be slow.
I ask your help, but only for his sake.
If you'd reprieve   him, let him leave:
you'll be to blame, if he does not awake.
Wake him, lady!'

'I'd like to see you damned to hell,
oh watchman, and your song as well!
Sleep, my love!
Your watching would be fine with me,
but waking him is villainy.
Sleep, my love!
Watchman, I do   nothing to you
but good, and you'll not grant me this request.
You wish for day,   to drive away
the joy of loving from my longing breast.
Sleep, my love!'

'I hope your wrath will disappear,
but still the knight can't linger here;

wake him, lady!
He trusted to my faithfulness
when I brought him to your caress;
wake him, lady!
Oh noble one,   if he's undone,
we too shall perish. I must warn
and sing and say: it now is day,
so wake him, or I'll wake him with my horn.
Wake him, lady!'

One often characterizes the compositions of a chivalric lyricist by showing how and to what extent they differ in content, mood, and form from the textbook example of the minnesong. The most distinctive characteristic of the songs of Ulrich von Lichtenstein, however, is that they themselves could serve as textbook illustrations of the genre, for, although Ulrich composed some years after the classical period of the minnesong, his works are fully as traditional and in every sense as chivalric as are those of Reinmar von Hagenau. Ulrich sings only of highborn ladies and, except for the pleasure he gets from the sight of his chosen one and the feeling of nobility which rises out of his suffering, his love is not rewarded. Nevertheless, the narrator is devoted to her and wishes to serve her in every way he can. And, even though some of these ways are rather far-fetched, there is no overt satire or parody. With regard to form Ulrich is quite sophisticated. Indeed, some of his songs display a virtuosity of rhyme and metrics exceeding that which was typical of the classical minnesingers. His favorite stanzaic patterns, however, are relatively simple, consisting frequently of a short rising song of four lines with alternating rhyme followed by an even shorter falling song, made up either of a single rhymed couplet or of three lines which rhyme *c c c*, *c b c*, or *c a c*. Structurally, his verse most resembles that of Neidhart with its lively rhythms and preference for short lines. Also reminiscent of Neidhart is the fact that most of his songs are dancing songs and that some are designated as summer or winter songs and have the appropriate nature introductions and moods. Although Ulrich never sings of peasants, one of his songs contains an argument between Dame Minne and the singer which at once recalls the arguments between peasants which Neidhart treats so dramatically. Fifty-eight songs and one *Leich* by Ulrich are extant. Of these twenty-seven are designated by the author as dancing songs, four are called singing songs, three are described as long melodies, two as departure songs, one as an outdoor dance song, and one as a ladies' dance song. Although none belong to the best of the minnesongs, all are technically superior, many present charming pictures and well-phrased ideas, and most have a fresh and lighthearted quality which seems to reflect a very interesting personality.

Not only the personality of Ulrich, but also the details of his life are better known than are those of any other minnesinger. In addition to such facts and impressions as can be gleaned from his songs there are eighty-eight official records of various kinds which mention him, a long autobiography in verse entitled *The Service of Ladies*, and an account in the rhyme chronicle of Ottokar of Styria, a poet and historian who was well acquainted with Ulrich. The latter was born in Styria in 1198 and died on the sixth of January of the year 1275 or 1276. He received the usual knightly education at the court of the margrave of Istria where he remained until the death of his father in 1219 made it necessary for him to assume responsibility for the extensive family properties. He was knighted in Vienna by Margrave Leopold in 1223, after which he travelled widely from tournament to tournament, winning considerable repute for his skill. In one season, according to the account in *The Service of Ladies*, he used up 307 spears. In 1241 he was appointed Lord High Steward of Styria and four years later was named marshall of the country. As one of the leading nobles of the land he took part in many historically important events. In 1251 he led his countrymen in a struggle against Hungarian domination, was accused of high treason in 1265 and spent twenty-six months in prison, took part in the crusade against the Prussians in 1267, and in 1270, as an old man, commanded an army in the invasion of neighboring Carinthia. These are a few of the high lights of an active and colorful life.

Ulrich's life was more interesting than his verse, and the most fascinating aspect of it was the way he managed to play in the real world of his time the romantic role of an Arthurian knight. For the chivalric deeds (which he performs for his lady-love) and knightly adventures which he recounts in *The Service of Ladies* are apparently factual. His life, as one critic describes it, was one long attempt to 'play a dream,' to make fact of fiction. And yet the times were such that his quixotism was not only accepted, but brought him honor and fame.

The first of the selections presented here is the introduction to *The Service of Ladies,* which was composed for the most part in 1255, although the songs interspersed in it are of earlier dates. The songs which follow the introduction are all contained in the autobiography and appear there with the titles given below. They were composed at various times during the decade beginning in 1232.

INTRODUCTION TO FRAUENDIENST

(Den guoten wîben sî genigen)

I greet the ladies, one and all,
though my reward was ever small
for serving them, I must confess.
What wealth of virtue they possess!
They're all the world can have of bliss,
for God made nothing else like this:
a noble woman. That is why
my praise of them must be so high.

You must admit it for it's true,
none give the honor that is due
to woman's goodness, though their praise
outstrips the light of summer days.
Where does the sunshine start and end?
If one on whom I can depend
can tell me that, then I'll declare
that he has travelled everywhere.

151

Their splendor lights up every land:
I do not know what distant strand
may mark the limit of their splendor.
Each word must change and be more tender,
each passing year must leave the earth
more fair, before a woman's worth
and goodness can be rightly heard,
completely told in song and word.

How can the story be completed
and all their virtues fully treated?
There is no end of what to say.
And when the world shall pass away,
the praise of women shall suffice
for poets up in paradise.
I fear, although I wish to speak
their praise, my thoughts are all too weak.

Women are pure, refined are they,
women are beautiful and gay,
women can still love's deepest pain,
women are never cruel and vain,
women make kind and noble men.
Well for him who deserves it when
the women greet him as a friend!
His sorrow and distress will end.

Women are rich in charm and grace.
To match their lovely form and face
is more than angels hope to do.
A woman, virtuous and true,
who has no faults of any kind,
must have an angel's heart and mind,
and like an angel seems to glow.
You have my word that this is so.

My praise is finished. Now I plan
to tell a tale as best I can

and pray to God as I begin
that I may interest you therein,
that all will listen as one should,
and all of you will think it good.
My labors then will satisfy.
I swear the story is no lie.

THIS IS A DANCE SONG, THE FIRST

(Wîbes güete   niemen mac)

No one can   tell all about
a woman's goodness. Days ago
my heart began   to blossom out.
She frees me from the cares I know
when, dressed in all her finery,
she walks along in front of me.
No angel is more fair than she.

By storm   a woman seized my heart
and I must always be her knight.
Her form   is lovely, every part;
her greeting fills me with delight.
All one could wish in her I find;
she leaves the others far behind
or I'm no judge of womankind.

You have shown   more friendliness
to me than ever I deserve.
You alone,   I now confess,
are she whom I shall ever serve.
I'm always happy on the day
I see you, more than I can say.
My heart is joyful then and gay.

All the cheer   that now is mine
I owe to no one else but you.
You are dear,   without design,

and I would serve you and be true.
If you'll permit, I'll show you how
I'll give away my freedom now.
I'll serve you faithfully, I vow.

THIS IS THE SECOND DANCE SONG

(In weiz wiech singe)

What shall I sing
about the night? I have no pleasure then.
The day must bring
fulfillment of my hopes—I see again.
Besides, its light
recalls the sight
of her I love, and is a true delight.

Well may he praise
the night who lies with love and shares its bliss,
but it dismays
my lonely heart. I hate the night for this
and praise the day,
for then I may
see her who drives my sorrows all away.

I celebrate
the day when first I saw my lady fair.
Since then I wait
for dawn with more and more of grief and care.
The night's to blame
that I became
so sad. But, Day, most blessed be thy name.

I am possessed
at night by grief and hosts of anxious fears.
They're put to rest
at once as soon as day's first light appears.
For then I know

that I must go
and watch in secret her whom I love so.

Oh gladly would
I praise the night, if it were not in vain,
or if I could
lie beside the one who brings me pain.
If it might be,
what ecstasy!
Alas, she will not grant this joy to me.

THIS IS A SONG OF DEPARTURE

(Wil iemen nâch êren die zît wol vertríben)

He who with honor would pass the time gaily,
would know true delight and enjoy himself daily
should faithfully serve a fair lady of station
for love's compensation.
Its sweetness and splendor
will only surrender
to those kind and tender.

Who courts as a knight and hopes for successes
must give heart and hand and the goods he possesses,
but love will reward him with wealth beyond measure,
so great is her treasure.
She honors, appeases
her pupil, and eases
his care as she pleases.

Knighthood demands both good manners and daring,
dishonor, deceit, and its fellows forswearing,
for God can't endure in his service the babble
of such wretched rabble.
His men must endeavor
to find honor ever
and infamy never.

Malice and coarseness, ill-nature and scheming
to neither the shield nor the helmet is seeming,
for knighthood's a roof that no evil can cover.
Its glance shall discover
the honorless fearful,
the frightened, half-tearful,
where brave men are cheerful.

High-minded ladies, remember with favor
the faithful companion whose heart will not waiver.
Love him in your thoughts and with all your affection
and thus your protection
may keep with the power
of love him each hour
from griefs that devour.

Through no fault of mine is the lady offended,
though I am her knight and for her have contended.
And now for protection from anger and sorrow
no shield can I borrow
but one: I still love her
and think kindly of her.
None else is above her.

I'll battle with patience her war-like resistance,
opposing her anger with guileless insistence.
Protected because I am faithful and loyal,
all falsehood I'll foil.
My battle attire
against her dread fire
is constant desire.

A DANCE SONG, THE NINETEENTH

(In dem luftesüezen meien)

In the warm and fragrant Maytime
when the woods are dressed in green

156

through the happy hours of daytime
all that loves in pairs is seen.
Every heart is filled with bliss,
and the spring was made for this.

Loving pairs in pleasant hours
soon are free from all distress;
in the hearts of both there flowers
all the season's happiness.
Sorrow Love cannot abide
when two loves are side by side.

When two loving hearts are plighted,
faithfully, without deceit,
when the two are so united
that their love must be complete,
they are joined by God, to capture
all that life can hold of rapture.

Constant love is *minne*. Truly
love and *minne* are the same.
I cannot distinguish duly
aught between them but the name,
nor can tell the two apart.
Love is *minne* in my heart.

Find a heart that does not vary,
constant love and constant mind,
then with grief you can be merry.
Constant love is good and kind,
and to constant hearts will give
constant pleasure while they live.

If I ever find enduring
love, then I would surely be
always loyal, with it curing
all the cares that come to me.
Faithless love will never do,
I must have a love that's true.

There is a noticeable similarity in mood and style between the songs of Ulrich and those of the Swiss count, Kraft von Toggen- burg, all of whose seven songs present the plaints of a lover whose high-born lady does not reward his service. Like Ulrich, however, Kraft manages to be rather cheerful despite his lack of success. Although his lyrics present nothing really new with regard to content, style, or form, still considered together, they possess enough that is distinctive to give them a particular character. All have a nature introduction and employ as symbols only objects of nature; all have a lightly melancholy tone; all are marked by simple and direct expression; and it is probable that all were composed as dancing songs. Three of the songs have forms which are not much more complicated than those used by *Spielleute*. If in the song, 'He Who Has a Mind for Pleasure,' the first two lines and the second two respectively are combined, a four-line stanza results which is made up of three long lines with caesuras and a shorter line—a common folksong form. The simile of the lady's lips and the rose, which the poet develops so well, also occurs frequently in folksongs.

There were three Swiss counts of this name—father, son, and grandson—but only the first two can be considered with regard to the authorship of the poems. The father, who appears in records from 1240 to 1254, was a strong and aggressive noble- man who was constantly involved in feuds with his neighbors. Little more is known of the son than that his name appears in a document of the year 1260. One would like to believe that it was the warlike parent who composed the tender and appealing songs.

HE WHO HAS A MIND FOR PLEASURE

(Hat ieman ze fröiden muot)

He who has a mind for pleasure,
come and meet us at the greening lime,
for its blooming summer treasure
crowns its leafy shade about this time.
We hear the notes of little birds resounding as they sing,

which cause the thoughts of loving hearts toward lofty heights
among the clouds to swing.

On the heath are blooms and flowers;
he for whom the May can lessen grief
there finds joy for gloomy hours.
Could love's sorrow offer me relief!
I'd be high in spirit and be rich in happiness,
if a pure and noble lady only would not laugh at my distress.

Laugh away, but don't destroy
with your laughing, lips so rosy red,
my good fortune and my joy,
which your laughter should increase instead.
The May and all the blossom's beauty could not give my mind
so much of happiness as could your laughter, if you meant it
to be kind.

Flowers, foliage, hill and dale,
and the May-time's summer-sweet delight
likened to the rose are pale
which my lady wears. The sun so bright
grows dim within my eyes when I behold the roses gay
which blossom from her little mouth as bloom the roses from
the dews of May.

Whoever gather roses here
rejoices in the way their beauty glows,
but of the roses I've been near,
none can compare with one imposing rose.
Whatever roses may be plucked within the valley there,
whene'er she laughs her red lips form a rose a thousand,
thousand times as rare.

Kraft's songs resemble those of his fellow countryman, Hesse
von Reinach, who also composed lover's plaints in the classical
tradition. Although the latter's expressions of sorrow are more

pronounced than Kraft's, they are to a certain extent cancelled out by his jocular exclamations, and it can be assumed that the poet did not expect to be taken very seriously. Only two of Hesse's lyric poems are extant: one is a plaint with the conventional description of the charms of the lady, the other is a spring song which invites the young people to come outdoors to play and requests the lady to make the narrator happy, too. The author was a clergyman of the minor nobility who is mentioned in various records from 1234 to 1275, first as a lay-priest, later as a canon at the monasteries of Beromünster and Zofingen, finally as prior at Werd, not far from Zürich. He was an energetic and influential cleric who not only wrote love verse, but also took part in the political activities of his day.

HEARTACHE AND DESPAIR

(Klagelîche nôt)

Heartache and despair
love has given me
when she bid me bear
this my longing plea
where I'll be destroyed and soon expire.
Ho, love and love's desire!
You have brought too much of pain and passion's fire.

Cheeks, so red and white,
soft and graceful chin,
eyes, serene and bright,
lovely brow and skin:
these she has who threatens health and life.
Oh delightful wife,
with your charm expel my grief and inner strife!

Gentle comforter,
strengthen now my heart
and your love confer
for which I burn and smart.

From the fire of love I suffer pain and dread.
Hey there, lips of red!
If you won't console me, I shall soon be dead.

In the late twelfth century and the thirteenth century the art of
poetic and musical composition was taught to young noblemen
as a normal part of an aristocrat's education. Songs of courtly
love were composed not only by priests, such as Hesse, but also
by royalty: Emperor Heinrich vi, King Wenzel ii of Bohemia,
and Konradin, King of Jerusalem and Duke of Swabia. Kon-
radin was born in Bavaria on March 25, 1252 as the son and heir
of Emperor Konrad iv. After the latter's death Konradin lived
with his mother in Swabia until 1267 when he led an army into
Italy in order to win back the crown of Sicily which he had
inherited from his father, but which had been given by Pope
Urban iv to Charles of Anjou. After initial military successes
the young king was defeated by Charles and was brought to
Naples where on August 23, 1268 he was executed. With his
death the Hohenstaufen family came to an end.

   The two songs of Konradin which are extant were probably
composed while he was still in Germany, that is, when he was
fourteen or fifteen years of age. They have been identified as
Swabian dance songs. The meaning of the question in line one
of the first poem is that the singer cannot regret the death of the
flowers as winter comes because his pangs of love are so intense.
The reference at the end of the second song to the poet's youth
and his inability to understand courtly love gives an impression
of touching sincerity.

SHALL I LAMENT

(Sol ich nu klagen)

Shall I lament   the flower?   Where is such great distress
compared to mine?   I burn in flames intense.
My courage spent,   I cower,   bare of happiness.
Her lips so fine   have robbed me of my sense.

How shall I ever win such joy as this?
The lady whom I've always praised above them all
will let me fall   in longing for a kiss.

If she'd receive   the loyalty   my heart has felt
for her alone,   then I'd be free of care.
She ought to grieve   because of me   and how she's dealt
to make me moan   so long, the lady fair,
that she has left me sad in heart and mind,
and that I've served her faithfully and been misled.
My joy is dead,   to me she'll not be kind.

I THINK WITH PLEASURE OF THE FLOWERS

(Ich fröi mich manger bluomen rôt)

I think with pleasure of the flowers
which May will bring to us again.
They've suffered many bitter hours:
the winter caused them grief and pain.
But May for sorrow gives us mirth,
rewards us with delightful days
      and fills with joy the waiting earth.

What good has summer ever done,
and summer days, so long and fair?
My only help may come from one
who is the cause of my despair.
If she'll but make my spirits rise,
then she'll be acting as she should,
      to give me joy instead of sighs.

If I should leave my Love tomorrow,
my happiness would surely end.
Alas, I think I'd die of sorrow,
for, Lady, I can't comprehend
the love of courtly chevaliers.
Love's made me pay distressingly
      for being such a child in years.

Although a composition by a nobleman was much more likely to survive than was a song by a *Spielmann* or goliard, still many songs by aristocrats were lost. And some which were not lost became separated from their composers, who remain anonymous. The three songs by unknown authors which appear below are all quite simple in style and content, and might have been composed by a *Spielmann*, goliard, middle-class singer, or cleric. They are given here because, despite their simplicity, they have an air of chivalry. The first is definitely of the thirteenth century, the other two received their final form either at the end of the thirteenth century or at the beginning of the fourteenth century. 'I Love Her' is one of the best songs of its period, and the mere repetition of 'I Love' is as effective with a modern reader as it was with a medieval listener. The song, 'See, in Honor's Land Appears Such Bliss,' is a bit more sophisticated, but, except for the reference to 'honor's land,' has the same timelessness and universal appeal. The mention in it of the wine of Cypress shows an influence of the 'Song of Solomon.' The third song is somewhat dated by its metaphors; however, the expression rings true and the sentiment is sincere.

I LOVE HER

(Siu ist mir liep und liebet mir für alliu wîp)

I love her! Oh I love her more than all the rest,
more than my life, my soul itself, I love her best.
I love with all my heart and could not love her more;
a lovelier was never born than is the woman I adore.

SEE, IN HONOR'S LAND APPEARS SUCH BLISS

(Awe, waz wunnen schinet in der eren lande)

See, in honor's land appears such bliss,
where the lover gives himself to love;
no other earthly joys compare with this,
for there's the love we've all been dreaming of.

Fear is vanquished there, no heart is faint
and love may go to love without restraint,
then one will whisper, taste of joy, recline
and drink unmixed the precious Cyprian wine.

OH HEART'S ONE LOVE, OH HEART'S ONE PAIN

(Ach herzeliep, ach herzeleit)

Oh heart's one love, oh heart's one pain,
oh life's most lovely loss and gain,
oh hyacinth, oh balsam dew,
oh sweetest sugar cane are you
of my life and of my heart;
from the world I'm set apart,
and by your sorcery.
The wonder conquers me,
till I am timid and resigned.
Soul and body, heart and mind
have no life that is their own,
since they no other love have known
but that they give to you alone.

The last significant composer of traditional minnesongs was
Wizlaw III, Prince of Rügen, who was born about the year 1268.
He was a member of the Slavic family which had ruled over the
Baltic island of Rügen and the neighboring mainland since their
Christianization and was closely related to other ruling houses
of the north. The singer's mother was a daughter of the Duke
of Braunschweig-Lüneburg, his brother, Jaromar, became ruler
of the bishopric of Kammin, a sister became queen of Norway,
and a nephew became Duke of Pomerania. After the death of
his father in 1302 Wizlaw shared the throne with his brother,
Sambor, until the latter's death two years later, at which time
he became the sole ruler of the principality. His reign was a
troubled one. He was threatened on the one hand by the rising
power of his largest city, Stralsund, and on the other by the

territorial ambitions of Denmark to the west and Brandenburg to the south. After years of internal and foreign war an unsettled peace was established and Wizlaw devoted his final years to the building up of his impoverished and war-torn land. He died in 1325 and left no heir. Rügen was ruled for a time by the Duke of Pomerania, but soon both lands were swallowed up by Brandenburg.

Wizlaw, according to one account, was 'a knightly gentleman, a politician of dubious talents and an even worse financier.' He was interested in science and the arts and associated much with scholars and poets, among whom was the middle class singer, Frauenlob, one of whose songs praises the noble character of the prince. Fourteen minnesongs and thirteen *Sprüche* by Wizlaw are extant. The *Sprüche* are chiefly concerned with moral and religious matters and may have been influenced by Reinmar von Zweter. They were probably composed before the minnesongs. The latter are much superior and represent a sort of Indian summer of the classical minnesong.

Wizlaw's characteristic note in the minnesongs is an optimistic and happy one. Although he sang of love's sorrows as well as its joys, his pain is always lightened by hope and never approaches despair. He sings of the joys of love in a frankly sensual manner which sometimes recalls that of Walther von der Vogelweide. There is charm in the best of Wizlaw's verse even for the modern reader; however, his music is generally superior to his verse and belongs to the best which the German minnesong has produced.

Structurally, Wizlaw's minnesongs are composed of an *Aufgesang* and an *Abgesang* which sometimes ended with a repeat of the *Stollen* melody. In most instances there are three stanzas. Since minnesongs, except those of the earliest period, traditionally have three or more stanzas, one may assume in the case of three of Wizlaw's four shorter songs that stanzas have been lost.

The single one-stanza minnesong that is probably complete is the one which begins: 'With my faithfulness would I adorn thee.' It is a simple and sincere declaration of love which produces such an impression of unity and completeness that one cannot imagine what the poet would have left to say in other stanzas. He addresses the lady directly, there is no hint of a performance or an audience, and one feels that, if any of Wizlaw's songs were intended for a particular person, it would be this one. It is perhaps significant that Wizlaw uses the word 'faithfulness' here and in no other song.

The following song below, 'The Fields No More Are Bare,' describes a village green in May, bright with colors of leaves, flowers, birds, and the gay spring costumes, decked with garlands of flowers, of those who have gathered there for a dance. The cheeks of the ladies are like rubies on the snow and the whole colorful scene reminds the singer of a magnificent tapestry. It is no wonder that he thinks of his lady and the delights of her love. Technically the work is quite interesting. The stanzas have a *Stollen* rhyme of *a a a b* and an *Abgesang* rhyme of *d d e e e*, thus the rhyme of the *Abgesang*, with the addition of a line, is just the reverse of that of the *Stollen*.

The song, 'Come To Us Delightful May,' presents a winter scene and is rather unique among the winter songs of the minnesingers. Those composed by the penniless wandering minstrels are often quite gloomy and reflect their own sufferings from the harsh elements. But Wizlaw, although he voices the usual complaint about the cold, is chiefly distressed because in winter the women conceal their pretty dresses with heavy, drab coats. For the most part he is well satisfied with winter, since he finds the long nights of love to be a more than adequate compensation for the loss of the delights of summer. These songs of consummated love are, of course, rather unusual in the minnesong tradition and ordinarily deal only with knights and peasant girls. The object of Wizlaw's affection, however, is a lady. Metrically the song is distinguished for its very effective use of the monometer line and its ingenious linking of stanzas by rhyming the last word of one stanza with the first word of the following one.

In 'The Fields and Forests, Far and Near' Wizlaw once more sings of the joys rather than of the sorrows of love, and does so with exuberance and baroque extravagance. He employs his most highly involved *Ton*, one which is almost unsurpassed in complexity, even in a period when poets especially prided themselves on metrical virtuosity. From the standpoint of poetry alone one might well object that such virtuosity must seem pretentious and detract from the effectiveness of the work. However, it must be remembered that a minnesong is sung and, since it is communicated through a double medium, it cannot be compared to a non-composed poem any more than an opera libretto should be compared to a drama. Libretti need to be exaggerated in order to stand out from the music, and the virtuosity of a minnesong often gave the performer excellent opportunities for effective and varied expression. The mention of hills in the nature introduction of the song suggests that it may have been composed on the island of Rügen. The mainland area of Wizlaw's principality consisted of a lowland plain.

The two May songs, 'I Greet You, May, and Grant You Praise and Honor' and 'At Break of Day,' are chiefly distinctive for their bold reference to the goal of the singer's frankly sexual desires, a goal which traditionally is carefully veiled with polite, but suggestive ambiguities. In the latter song there is even the most unconventional threat that the singer may resort, if necessary, to sovereign prerogatives. The best element in the former song is the simple and appealing portrayal of the lady's feeling of pride in knowing that she is beautiful in her fine clothes and that everyone is admiring her. Of particular interest in 'At Break of Day' are the brief description of a tournament and the subsequent festivities and the clever, if slightly naughty, play on the word 'jousting.'

Although Wizlaw in most respects followed the accepted minnesong tradition, he sometimes deviated from it, as has already been indicated. His most radical departure from the minnesong of the classical period is seen in his fall song, 'Harvest Brings a Rich Supply.' The single extant stanza, which is not quite complete, describes in a realistic, unadorned manner the simple joys of harvest time: the beer and wine, the fat geese and pigs, the cackling of chickens and the fishing in the brooks. Although one can assume that the missing stanzas introduced a love element, there is little here of the sophisticated expression of the conventional minnesong. There are two explanations for the distinctive tone of the song. One deals with the nature of the harvest festival itself. Although its origins are as remote in the Germanic past as those of the spring festival, it was never fully adopted and refined by courtly society and was treated only rarely by courtly singers until the latter part of the fourteenth century when the Monk of Salzburg began to compose. The harvest song, therefore, remained to some extent a forthright peasant song, even in the hands of a sophisticated composer. The tone of the song can also be explained on the basis of literary influence, for Wizlaw obviously drew from a well-known drinking song (which appears in the following chapter) by the Swiss singer, Steinmar. The latter's song has a rough and earthy flavor which could have been transmitted in part to Wizlaw's verses.

WITH MY FAITHFULNESS WOULD I ADORN THEE

(Ich partere dich durch mîne vrowen)

With my faithfulness would I adorn thee,
since my eyes first saw thee in thy beauty.
Love, be mine, and never let me mourn thee,
thou paragon of virtue and of duty.
Oh none can merit thy affection
but God who grants thee his protection;
this I too must have or soon must perish
of love for thee whom I would hold and cherish.

THE FIELDS NO MORE ARE BARE

(De erde ist untslozen)

The fields no more are bare,
the flowers are everywhere,
we go to join them there
in haste with spirits high.
The birds sing noisily
from every bush and tree,
of ice and snow now free,
they're lords of earth and sky.
The woods have lost their chill,

in leafy groves we thrill
with all the joys of May.
Winter, keep away!
The summer has come to stay.

To wreaths the flowers are wound,
with golden threads are bound.
'In blooms so richly gowned,
come ladies, to the field.'
Their cheeks are all aglow,
like rubies on the snow,
the spring has made them so.
What cloth this scene would yield
if woven on a loom!
They all are free of gloom,
red lips will get their due
upon the green anew;
their pleasures surely won't be few.

There many a heart in vain
is kindled and is slain
by love's consuming pain.
Beware, Oh Love, beware!
If thou show no concern,
who then to thee will turn?
Joy shouldst thou never spurn.
Be not so proud, take care
to let thy loyal knight
partake of love's delight
and thou shalt never be,
sweet lady, far from me.
This is my pledge to thee.

(Meyie scône kum io tzuo)

Come to us, delightful May,
long have you remained away,
asleep.
The women wear such dreary clothes,
this is chief among my woes.
They keep
all their pretty dresses from the weather,
but you, fair May, can change this altogether.
They're hidden by the coats they wear
(Winter, this is most unfair)
from cold.

Hold,   O Winter, frosts that chill
and I'll be your vassal still.
Forbear!
It's a fault you cannot hide,
making us remain inside.
I share
all the heavy trials that you measure,
but I am silenced by a single pleasure.
It's the long and happy nights
with their amorous delights
so dear.

Here   I stay and shall not go,
for my lady's winsome glow
makes me
happy as a blissful boy.
God, take not away this joy,
I beg Thee.
When she gently calls and I awaken
my every member then with joy is shaken
and I exclaim: 'Oh rosy lips,
how my heart with rapture skips!
God bless you.'

THE FIELDS AND FORESTS, FAR AND NEAR

(Der walt und angher lyt ghebreyt)

The fields and forests, far and near,
in brightly colored dress appear.
Hear   the sweet notes from leafy bowers,
the birds are singing a pretty air
with happy spirits everywhere.
Fair   is the sight of trees and flowers,
clear,   dear,   sincere   are the Maytime's faces.
Graces,   places
of charm I see with joy o'er hills and meadows wending,
far extending.

The wonders of the fields in May
are fair as on creation's day.
They   can't compare with a new creation,
that drives away each pain and sigh,
a lovely lady, sweet and shy.
I   see in her my true salvation.
Sight,   might,   delight,   all on me bestowing.
Glowing,   showing
kindness to me, Oh darling, my love you must cherish,
else I shall perish.

Oh Love, your bounty is so great
that I could die from this joyful state.
Fate   has made you my well of gladness
and I am wholly in your power:
grant me many a happy hour,
shower   with blessings, banish sadness.
Your name   and fame   I proclaim,   knowing I shall never,
ever   endeavour
to part from that which frees from care and brings me bliss.
Wizlaw, sing this!

I GREET YOU, MAY, AND GRANT YOU
PRAISE AND HONOR

(Wol dan her meyie ich ghebe ûch des de hulde)

I greet you, May, and grant you praise and honor,
my lady comes in all the springtime color
and finery which you have urged upon her;
when snow and ice were here, her clothes were duller.
She's opened up her chest
and donned her very best,
now here is she
as if to say: 'Just look and see,
you men and women, look at me.'

My lady knows I sing of Maytime splendor,
but I would rather listen to her speaking;
her charms are manifold, her heart is tender,
of thousands she's the one whom I've been seeking.
So fair is she alone
beneath the heaven's throne;
there's none as nice,
as kind this side of paradise;
so sing her praise, is my advice.

If she should seem to welcome my advances,
then I may hope to see my love requited,
and should I read my wishes in her glances,
upon a bed we soon would be united.
It easily may be
the lady will agree
on nothing less
and I shall hear a loving 'Yes,'
and then find endless happiness.

(De voghelîn)

At break of day
the little birds salute the May
with merry songs and bright array
and thanks for happy hours.
The fields are bright
with blossoms: yellow, red, and white,
a wealth of color greets the sight
from leaves and grass and flowers.
The meadow lies
so fair beneath the summer skies,
a feast for men's and women's eyes
of beauties without number.
What May unfolds
the sun with splendor shapes and moulds;
may he be happy now who holds
his loved one here in slumber.

But look and see
how gay the tournament can be
with jousts and splendid pageantry
and afterwards the dances.
Make haste to share
the many pleasures everywhere
and you will find an end to care
in pretty ladies' glances.
A cavalier
should seek the love of ladies here;
there's one, I think, who holds me dear.
If I only knew it!
If she confessed,
I'd throw myself upon her breast
and there'd be jousting then with zest,
but she would never do it.
I act as though

my suit had brought me joy, I know,
and hide with merriment my woe,
but this is only acting.
My dear, say 'Yes,'
receive me now with tenderness
and set me free from my distress;
I find you most distracting.
Who knows this age?
Who knows how love engenders rage?
Long have I waited for my wage;
Oh free me from this fire!
You vacillate
and drive me into such a state
that I might well refuse to wait,
and seize what I desire.

HARVEST BRINGS A RICH SUPPLY

(Der herbest kumpt uns riche nuoch)

Harvest brings a rich supply,
man, your wants to satisfy;
many gifts before us lie,
all that feeds and quickens.
Beer and mead and golden wine,
cattle, geese, well-fattened swine,
these delights are yours and mine,
flocks of noisy chickens.
All that grows upon the earth,
man, was given you at birth
and the water's fishes.
Thus we can have a happy life,
for God... [missing]

10

NEW DIRECTIONS IN THE COURTLY LYRIC

Although the influence of the classical and pre-classical minne-song on the thirteenth century was significant, the strongest influence to be exerted by courtly singers was that of Walther and Neidhart. Their songs and the *Spielmann* songs from which they drew provided new material and new attitudes for the courtly lyric and encouraged a closer relationship between literature and life. The new directions of the verse of the century were mainly toward an increased realism which gave it different values, expressions, and symbols and frequently led to parody and satire. Walther had many followers in his use of courtly verse forms to tell of the love of a village maiden, to discuss political affairs, or to advise the youth. Neidhart's peasant dances and parody of chivalric manners were imitated and echoed by his contemporaries and successors. But much of that which was new in the courtly lyric was doubtless taken from the popular songs of the *Spielleute*: animal stories, fairy tale material, fabulous Oriental creatures, problems of village society, Marian themes, and harvest festivals. It was doubtless the influence of the *Spielleute* as well as that of Walther and Neidhart which caused an increase in the amount of humorous verse, and much of the humor was the result of ridicule of ideals and themes which a previous generation had taken very seriously.

Very much in keeping with the spirit of the times were the songs of the hero of the Venus Mountain ballad and Wagner's opera, Tannhäuser. He was born about the year 1200 as the younger (and therefore propertyless) son of Bavarian or Austrian nobility. He appears in no historical records and our knowledge of him is derived solely from personal references in his works. These tell of an adventurous, exuberant, and wastrel life. In the early part of his career, Tannhäuser was a protege of Friedrich II of Austria and his two sons, Heinrich and Konrad. From Friedrich the singer received extensive properties, including a residence in Vienna, which enabled him to carry on a gay existence at the court, interrupted by his participation in the crusade of 1228-29 and the Cyprian War two years later. With the death of Friedrich in 1246 Tannhäuser's carefree life was over, and the hardships of the penniless minstrel began. For he long before had wasted away the property which Friedrich had given him. From then on until his death around 1266 Tannhäuser wandered from court to court, supporting himself meagerly with his songs.

The style and general content of Tannhäuser's love songs, *Leiche* and *Sprüche* is courtly, but one can readily see that the singer does not take the courtly ethic or the ideal of *minne* seriously. In a humorous and often ironic manner he parodies chivalric themes: his grand lady turns out to be a simple peasant girl, his knightly deeds are exaggerated to the impossible, his languishing lover becomes ridiculous. Two contrasting moods predominate in his works, the one a jovial affirmation of the life of the senses, the other a sad regret that such good times as he had experienced should end. Most of his love songs and five of his six *Leiche* are composed to dance rhythms, not to those of courtly dances, but to those of lively, even tumultuous village dances. The dance songs, like those of Neidhart (by whom he was influenced), are divided into summer songs and winter songs.

Tannhäuser was by nature a realist, not only in his burlesques of outworn themes, but also in his keen interest in the world about him. The songs of no other courtly singer contain so much factual and detailed information as do his. They reveal, too, a broad knowledge of literature and contain allusions to Arthurian legends, Germanic heroic verse, and even to classical figures. Tannhäuser's familiarity with the *Spielmann* lyric is seen in his use of riddles as well as his treatment of peasants. Only two of his songs deal with courtly love and even there in a rather off-hand manner. The singer is not one to waste his time with plaints about wooing in vain, his suit is more often than not successful. Tannhäuser was obviously not interested, either immediately or symbolically, in the ethical aspects of courtly love. Nor is there idealism revealed in his one crusade song. In it he tells of his experiences and hardships, but says little about any religious purpose or goal. He was, however, capable of sincere religious feeling and expression, as several of his poems demonstrate.

In the song, 'My Lady Wishes to Reward,' Tannhäuser parodies the extravagant promises made by lovers in the earlier minnesong and ridicules the chivalric idea of service to a noble lady. He here reveals his most characteristic mood. The second song, 'How Delightful is this Lovely Day,' is not typical of Tannhäuser and the question has been raised as to whether he is really the author. It may be that this song was the cause of his becoming associated with the Venus Mountain legend. It is also possible, however, that the song was altered in the process of oral transmission to conform with an already established folk tradition such as appears in the Tannhäuser ballad.

MY LADY WISHES TO REWARD

(Mîn frowe diu wil lônen mir)

My lady wishes to reward
my service and my loyalty.
Let's thank her, all with one accord,
for having been so kind to me.
I only need to cause the Rhine
to flow no more through Coblenz land
and she will grant a wish of mine.
She'd also like some grains of sand
from out the sea where sets the sun,
then she'll give heed to my request.
She wants a star, the nearest one
will do, it need not be the best.
My love is strong,
whate'er her song

I will not think she does me wrong,
my own.
To God alone
and no one else is this fair lady known.

If from the moon I steal the glow,
then may I have this noble wench.
And she'll reward me well, I know,
if 'round the world I dig a trench.
If like an eagle I might fly,
then would she welcome my advances
(that is, if none could soar so high),
or if I broke a thousand lances
within a day, as did the sire
of Parzival to win the prize,
she'd gladly do what I desire,
't will cost me plenty otherwise.
My love is strong
whate'er her song
I will not think she does me wrong,
my own.
To God alone
and no one else is this fair lady known.

If I the Elbe's waters bound,
I'd be rewarded; could I make
the Danube flow without a sound,
she'd love me well for custom's sake.
A salamander I must bring
to her from searing fire and flame,
then she will grant me anything
that any loving knight might claim.
When I can turn aside the rain
and snow, I've often heard her say,
and make the summer wax and wane,
then I shall have a lover's pay.
My love is strong,
whate'er her song

I will not think she does me wrong,
my own.
To God alone
and no one else is this fair lady known.

HOW DELIGHTFUL IS THIS LOVELY DAY

(Ez ist hiute eyn wunnichlicher tac)

How delightful is this lovely day!
Now care for me who over all disposes,
that I may ever live with blessing
and may do penance for my worldly blindness.
For he indeed will be my stay
and through His aid my soul secure reposes.
May I be healed of all transgressing
and may I yet obtain God's loving kindness.
Grant me a will which shall not bend
and which deserves His love so well
that God may well reward me!
May I but have a happy end,
and may my soul in rapture dwell,
a gentle death afford me.
May I be saved by purity,
that hell may be no danger.
What I require, give unto me,
that I to highest joy be not a stranger.
Here must I have no family,
that friends I may have yonder
who take such pleasure in my songs
that I shall be renowned among the knights
        who heavenward wander.

Of the many disciples and imitators of Walther von der Vogel-
weide among the younger generation of the early thirteenth
century, the most prolific was Reinmar von Zweter. There are
no historical records of this singer, and all that we know of him

is that which can be gleaned from his songs. He was born in the Middle Rhine area about the year 1200, but grew up in Austria, perhaps at the court of Leopold VI and Friedrich II. It is quite likely that he became acquainted with Walther at this time. From Austria Reinmar went to Bohemia, where he spent at least four years at the court of King Wenzel I. A wandering life followed, which was interrupted by fairly lengthy stays at Meissen and Mainz. He died about the year 1260. According to the tradition of the Master Singers, he was blind.

One religious *Leich* by Reinmar is extant and 229 to 253 one-stanza songs, the latter number including all those of disputed authorship. Most of the songs are composed in the same *Ton* and, with few exceptions, are *Sprüche* rather than minnesongs. Like Walther, Reinmar was very much interested in the social and political situation of his times. He, too, opposed the domination of the papacy and advocated a strong empire. He was also concerned with religious and spiritual matters, to which many of his songs are devoted. Almost all of Reinmar's compositions, even those dealing with love, are strongly didactic. Often, following the tradition of Spervogel, he clothes his moral teachings in the form of animal fables. Other *Spielmann* influences can be seen in his use of riddles and fairy tale material.

Reinmar viewed the world about him as a clear-eyed realist and described it in a direct, rather blunt, and sometimes humorous manner. He possessed little lyrical talent and, judging from the fact that most of his songs employ the same melody, probably even less talent as a composer. However, despite these limitations, he is second only to Walther as a composer of *Sprüche*. With regard to the history of the German lyric, Reinmar is important for having introduced the courtly love song and the *Spruch* into Bohemia and for the influence which he exerted on later Bohemian singers.

The song, 'Upon this Earth Once Lived a Maid,' is one of many songs in praise of the Virgin Mary. She and the miracle of the immaculate conception were favorite subjects for medieval singers, secular as well as clerical. The themes reached the height of their popularity among lyric poets with the sixteenth century Master Singers, among whom Reinmar von Zweter was a favorite and influential model. The song, 'Sir Cock, I Grant to You the Prize,' might have been composed by a *Spielmann* except for the relatively sophisticated metrical pattern and rhyme scheme. It is indicative of the changing times and of the decline of the cult of chivalric love that a knight should treat women so harshly as Reinmar does in this humorous song. The fact that he uses the same melody for this stanza as for the Marian song demonstrates the close connection between religious and secular verse and the fact that melodies moved readily from one to the other. The hymn, 'Salve Regina, Mater Misericordiae,' has been attributed to Reinmar by medieval anthologists, but the authorship has been questioned by some modern scholars. It is almost a paraphrase of the Latin Marian antiphon which was probably written by Hermannus Contractus, who died in 1054. The Latin version was the subject of sermons from 1100 on, and soon became a favorite with hymn writers who wrote sermonizing hymns meditating on each phrase of the antiphon in separate stanzas. Reinmar's song doubtless used the melody of the original, which has been preserved. The last selection by Reinmar, 'O God and Thy Eternal Reign,' consists of the first two segments of Reinmar's single *Leich*, a rather long work in which he sings of divine love.

UPON THIS EARTH ONCE LIVED A MAID

(Es wont ein magt ûff erden hie)

Upon this earth once lived a maid;
she sent her messengers   and for the Son of God they prayed:
her innocence, her modesty,   her humbleness, her purity
with all their power God did ask
that He would give to her   the pure and most exalted task
that she, a maid, might bear Him,   as an angel promised it
should be.
And when her messengers the news had heard,
and when they brought to her the joyous word,
the Holy Spirit showed in her His might.

She saw the Child, this maiden blessed,
just as It lay beneath her breast
till It was born. How can we pay her right?

SIR COCK, I GRANT TO YOU THE PRIZE

(Hêr Han, ich wil iu siges jehen)

Sir Cock, I grant to you the prize,
you're really very brave   as I have seen with my own eyes.
You're master in your house   though you've more wives than
                                            most think necessary.
As for myself, I've only one.
She's soured all my thoughts   and spoiled all my fun,
she wears the pants, you know,   and loudly scolds whenever
                                            I am merry.
If I had two of her, I'd laugh no more,
my joys would disappear, if I had four,
I'd pine away, if I had eight,
they'd surely be the death of me.
Sir Cock, keep well the bravery
that rules a dozen hens and frees their mate.

SALVE REGINA, MATER MISERICORDIAE

(Salve regina, mater misercordie)

'Salve regina, mater misericordiae!
This greeting do I bring to thee, thou queen most high!
I hail thee, lady of charity, this day!'
Only she may thus be greeted, she alone,
for none like she is on the earth or heaven's throne,
she guides the stranger on his lonely way.
Though you may journey early or late,
she blesses you and never will forsake you.
The power of our queen is great,
rejoice, therefore, and let not fear o'ertake you.
Come soon, I counsel everyone,

for late remorse is less reward to win,
whatever child of man has done
bring her your pain for she can conquer sin.
The judge she carries on her arm
will grant her each request,
and she'll protect you from all harm.
Fear no alarm,
the queen of mercy still can charm
and guide all for the best.

O GOD AND THY ETERNAL REIGN

(God und dyn êwen êwykit)

O God and Thy eternal reign,
supported by a Trinity,
may Thou be praised, because our pain
was driven forth by one of three,
and this One is a son to Thee.
Through Thy command this earth He trod,
and for our soul's salvation bled,
He died as man and not as God,
He died in human grief and dread.
His death has gained us life instead.

Quite different in tone from traditional chivalry as well as the
humorous satire of Tannhäuser, or the rather prosaic didacticism
of Reinmar von Zweter, are the songs of Burchard von Hohen-
fels. Burchard belonged to a knightly family which took its
name from the Castle of Hohenfels in Southern Swabia on Lake
Constance, one tower of which is still standing today. The poet
seems to have been a person of some means and importance and
not dependent on his songs for his livelihood. His name and
that of his brother Walther appear in various documents from
1216 to 1242: in the city of Ulm first as a witness to a document
by the Emperor Friedrich II, then frequently from 1222 to 1227
in connection with Friedrich's somewhat wanton son King

183

Heinrich VII, finally as a witness on the occasion of the investiture of the knight Albero von Spielberg by the Bishop of Constance.

Burchard's songs reveal a broad range of interests and moods. Like Walther he sings both of courtly love and love for a simple peasant girl. In the manner of Neidhart he composes summer and winter dance songs about villagers, but, unlike Neidhart, he does not make fun of them. As is Reinmar von Zweter, Burchard is concerned with problems dealing with local society and mores; he treats them, however, in a much more lyrical and interesting manner, often using the dialogue technique. Jollity and seriousness, frivolity and melancholy, joking and sadness, fantasy and practicality—all appear in his works and sometimes alternate within the same song. His most characteristic quality lies in the originality of his symbolism. This does not consist of stereotyped phrases, but of images drawn from his own life and interests or from the fabulous narratives of *Spielleute* and goliards: his heart sends his thoughts out on a hunt, he conceals himself from the pain of love behind high mountains and broad waters, the lark flees from the falcon, the fish struggles in the net, the bees follow their queen, the monkey is captivated by his image in the mirror, the unicorn sits in the maiden's lap. Burchard is a master of form, particularly of rhythm, and is skillful in his use of rhyme. Still the impression given is that of a talented amateur, composing and singing for his own pleasure and the entertainment of friends, rather than of a professional who has carefully studied his art.

The first song is a winter dance song which charms the reader with its light-hearted mood and lively meter, as well as with the innocent excitement felt by the peasant youth as his hands rest on the hips of his partner and the humorous warning at the end. The second is also a dance song, but what was to have been a dance in the open air ends up as a dance in a barn. A good example of Burchard's originality of symbol is contained in the metaphor of the earth being embraced and made pregnant by the warm rays of the summer sun and in the claim that the image of the girl has been engraved with hardest steel on the heart of the narrator. The last stanza is especially pleasing and commu-

nicates to the reader something of the thrill and pride which the
narrator feels as he describes his rustic sweetheart.

SUMMER IS GONE, WE MUST PLAY IN THE INN

(Wir sun den winter   in stuben enphâhen)

Summer is gone,   we must play in the inn;
children, come on,   for the dance will begin!
Just follow me
and we shall wink,   and smile as we blink,
and flirt merrily.

Gaily we'll glide   in a closely-pressed throng;
lay flute aside,   we'll begin with a song.
As we advance
hold up your train,   and with the refrain
we'll leap to the dance.

No one must lose   the prize of his pleasure,
each one must choose   his own beloved treasure,
and all will feel good.
However she trips,   keep your hands on her hips —
which excites as it should.

One cannot drive   the love from his heart;
in vain will he strive,   it will not depart.
Love without end:
howe'er it occurs!   it charms and it stirs
the thoughts of a friend.

Joyful, we've parted   from worrisome things;
all you faint-hearted,   now spread forth your wings,
but you must beware.
Those shy, smiling glances   with which she entrances
are bait for a snare.

185

(Dô der luft mit sunnen viure)

When the sun had warmed the air
with its rays from glowing fire
and the water gave its share
to refresh the earth, desire
with a secret, close embrace
made it pregnant. It revealed
fruits of joy in every place.
Look yourself upon the field!
Joy and freedom are unfurled
to be seen by all the world.

Tavern heat had chased us hence,
but we then were wet by rain.
One old woman, with some sense,
offered us a barn for grain.
Sadness was forgotten there,
sorrows all were put aside,
joy soon conquered every care
when the dance began to glide.
Joy and freedom are unfurled
to be seen by all the world.

Pretty barn-dance melodies
make the greatest troubles shrink,
lightly danced, with grace and ease.
Everyone began to think
of that so dear to one and all.
Who can hope for luck in this
finds a lover's grief is small:
happy thoughts can bring us bliss.
Joy and freedom are unfurled
to be seen by all the world.

Loving prattle, secret glancing
came from every lovely maid,

friendly jests and sly romancing:
so the pleasant game was played.
There did merry voices sound,
manners and delight combine.
Pretty girls were all around,
but the prettiest was mine.
Joy and freedom are unfurled
to be seen by all the world.

Oh, but how her beauty glows,
she's a picture of delight
when bedecked with blooms she goes,
all are gladdened by the sight,
heart and eye admire unstinted.
Joy she brings I can't conceal,
in my heart is she imprinted,
deeply as with hardest steel.
Joy and freedom are unfurled
to be seen by all the world.

Along with the increasing tendency to substitute village maidens
for noble ladies in courtly verse appeared another tendency
which was to erase the differences between them. One notices
this especially in the six songs which appear under the name of
Der von Buwenburg, who uses the terms 'lady' and 'woman'
interchangeably and is obviously not concerned one way or
another with the social station of his females. He was also
unconventional in his praise of the solid, material pleasures of
harvest time as opposed to the fleeting joys of spring. The song
below is a minnesong, but a somewhat unusual one. Although
the beauties of spring are described in the first stanza, it ends
with a reminder that fall is the season on which human happiness
depends. In the third stanza both the question as to who advised
God to separate the singer from his loved one and the method of
softening diamonds are new to the minnesong, although the
latter is mentioned in the long poem, 'The Younger Titurel.'
Der von Buwenburg is apparently the Konrad von Buwen-

burg who is spoken of in a Latin poem as having been an ancient choir director at the Swiss Monastery of Einsiedeln in 1314. He may also be the Konrad who appears in a document of 1255 together with his father, a Swabian nobleman.

(Waz ist daz liehte daz lûzet her vür)

What is the brightness that furtively spies
from the green and new-grown grass, as if it smiled
to win from us a greeting with a jest?
They are the flowers: I now recognize
spring by birds and other dwellers in the wild.
See how nature has to do her best
till each single thing
fills the day's demand.
God grant that fall a rich reward may bring,
for here the base of human joy must stand.

Were it not for hope, then I'd be dead
from her constant 'No' and 'I'll not act that way;'
she only hears from me a willing 'Yes.'
Often a lovely evening red
follows on a morning that is drab and gray;
so I serve her, hoping for success,
who for many a year
owes me a reward.
Ah, had I but won this lady dear,
the world would never see a gayer lord.

Diamonds, although very hard,
can be broken when they're drenched with blood of
goats;
thus might favor, urged by love, dispel
hate and win me her regard.
Who sat with God in council, cast the votes
parting her from me? No one can tell.

188

Love who dwells in right
banish grief and shame,
change my sorrow into joy; you have the might.
Then shall greater honor grace thy name.

Most of the forms and characteristics of the mid-thirteenth
century courtly lyric appear in the work of the Swabian noble-
man and cleric, Ulrich von Winterstetten. Ulrich composed
dance *Leiche*, *Minneleiche*, courtly village songs, dawn songs, and
other minnesongs. Although he composed some verses which
are almost as simple as those of a folksong, he preferred ingenious
and highly complicated metrical and rhyme patterns, excelling
all other aristocratic minnesingers in technical virtuosity. Ulrich
liked dance rhythms. Of his five *Leiche*, three announce them-
selves to be dance compositions and it is quite likely that the
other two were also performed at dances. Most of his forty
shorter lyrics, perhaps excepting only the five dawn songs, were
also intended to accompany dancing. Following the tradition of
dance songs, most of Ulrich's works have nature introductions,
divided evenly between summer songs and winter songs. His
treatment of love ranges from the regret of the peasant girl that
the local men do not know how to court properly to what at
first reading might seem to be the traditional plaint of the knight
with regard to the highborn lady. Like Buwenburg, Ulrich uses
the words 'woman' and 'lady' interchangeably and does not
emphasize the lofty station of his heroines. They are also more
human and individualistic and less symbolic than in the classical
minnesong. Because of this his minnesongs, although retaining
the conventional forms and expressions, begin to take on some-
thing of the spirit of the popular love songs of the *Spielleute* and
goliards. Some of his dialogue reminds one of popular verse,
for example when one fair lady expresses the medieval equivalent
of 'I'll bet you tell that to all the girls.' Ulrich's most character-
istic poetic device, the refrain, emphasizes the light, almost
frivolous nature of his rhythms and adds to the popular note.
Thirty-one of his songs have refrains which were repeated by
dancers and spectators between the stanzas sung by the chief

performer. Ulrich was quite familiar with courtly verse and, though no mere imitator, was probably influenced by Walther, Neidhart, Burchard, and Tannhäuser. His dawn songs are reminiscent of those of Wolfram.

Ulrich was the fourth of seven sons of Konrad von Schmalnegge and, on the maternal side, a grandson of the well-known Konrad von Winterstetten who was a counselor of King Konrad IV. The poet appears in documents which are dated from 1241 to 1280. In 1258 he is mentioned as a canon at Augsburg, although he probably never had a lasting residence there. It is possible that he lived at the ancestral castle of Tanne-Winterstetten, the ruins of which can still be seen. His songs were probably composed before the middle of the century.

The courtly village song below shows the general influence of Neidhart as well as that of another thirteenth century composer, Gottfried von Neifen. The song is intended to show the widespread fame of the singer and the effect of his art on female hearts. The lower social class to which mother and daughter belong is indicated in the original by their speech, which is colloquial and unsophisticated. The narrator's invective, 'You old leather wagon,' was a common term of abuse for old women. What distinguishes this song from many others of the same type is the quiet nobility of the peasant girl and her brave, though pathetic resolution to flee from her uncouth surroundings and follow her dreams in the search for a more meaningful existence.

IS THERE NOTHING PRETTY

(Ist iht mêre schoenes)

'Is there nothing pretty,'
spoke an ancient shrew,
'that nobleman can sing?
It's strange as it can be.
Oh, this awful ditty,
it pierces through and through
and makes my ears both ring:
this always angered me.

They howl his verses in the night and all day long
throughout this street,
and yet he never could compose a pretty song.
I hate this cheat;'
all this I heard her say.
'You old leather wagon, that's why you're so gray!'

A girl then spoke, 'How could
you hate him as you do?
For God's sake tell me this,
dear mother,' said the maid.
'And, if the song is good,
what harm is that to you,
since he does naught amiss
and never sounds dismayed?'
'I know that it was he who tried last year to take you,
on my cot;
and if this devil comes again, then I'll forsake you
on the spot;'
all this I heard her say.
'You old leather wagon, that's why you're so gray.'

'Kindest mother dear,'
the maiden answered so,
'think better, if you can,
for he is innocent.
Do not be severe,
and let the matter go;
you hate the worthy man
and songs he may invent.
I swear, it grieved him much that this occured to me.
It was his brother.'
The old one spoke, 'You haven't any modesty,
and no one other;'
all this I heard her say.
'You old leather wagon, that's why you're so gray.'

'If you can justify
and help such folks as he,'
the mother thus began,
'then you have been beguiled.
I wish that I knew why.
You are much too free
and love no upright man;
oh, most unhappy child!
Do you believe he'll dedicate to you the song
he'll soon begin?
You're not the prettiest to whom he did belong,
or whom he'll win;'
all this I heard her say.
'You old leather wagon, that's why you're so gray.'

She began to sing
artfully an air
from rosy lips and true,
the proud and lovely maid.
So sweetly she let ring
what drove away all care,
a song that she well knew,
for she was not afraid.
'Alas,' thus spoke the mother. 'What is on your mind?
You're leaving me!
The courtly songs have robbed you of your sense,
                                                I find.
You want to flee.'
She answered, 'Mother, yes,
to harvest, or to somewhere else, I guess.'

Like Ulrich von Winterstetten, the Swiss knight who appears
in manuscript as Sir Steinmar composed a variety of songs:
minnesongs, courtly village songs, summer and winter songs, a
fall song, and humorous parodies of dawn songs and chivalric
love in general. Unlike Ulrich he used, with one exception, very
simple *Töne*. Eight of his fourteen songs have a rising song which

consists of four lines with alternating rhyme and a falling song of from one to three rhymed couplets. For several songs he uses the rhyme scheme *a a b c c b* for the rising song, while the falling song is once more made up of from one to three couplets. As with most of the minnesingers, his favorite number of stanzas was three, with five in second place. Ten of his songs have nature introductions, of which six celebrate the summer, three the winter, and one the fall. Most of his compositions have refrains, which in some cases change slightly from stanza to stanza. Steinmar's simplicity of form, his use of refrains, his treatment of peasant courtship, and his frank revelation of the goal (not marriage) of that courtship, all give his work something of a *Spielmann* or goliard flavor—which is made more pronounced by his direct and rather blunt language as well as by his use of rural similes. He tells of a pig struggling in a sack and of a duck who dives to escape a falcon. The identity of Steinmar has not been definitely established. It is possible that he is the Berthold Steinmar who appears in documents from 1251 to 1294 and who was with Rudolf of Hapsburg in 1276 when he conquered Vienna.

The song given here is called a *Schlemmerlied* or glutton's song which celebrates the gastronomic joys of fall as opposed to the amorous pleasures of spring. Many such songs were composed by goliards and were popular up into the sixteenth century. Steinmar's work must have been well known for it was copied by several other poets.

SINCE SHE GIVES SO LITTLE PAY

(Sît si mir niht lônen wil)

Since she gives so little pay
whom I've sung in many a lay,
hear, my praises now
go to autumn, who will bring
rewards, and let the clothes of spring
fall from every bough.
It's an ancient tale they often tell;

that a lover is a wretched martyr, I know well.
Look, I've suffered in this strife;
I'll exchange it for a gaier, lusty life.

Autumn, I have been betrayed
and would like to give you aid
against the Maytime's splendor.
You protect from love's design.
Now that you've lost Gebewine,
take me, young and tender,
in his place, to be your loyal thane.
'Steinmar, see, that I shall do, if you can make it plain
that your praise will be as sweet.'
Fine, I'll sing a song to make all want to eat.

Autumn, hear how I would live:
landlord, fish! And you must give
us ten different brands,
geese and chickens, birds and swine,
peacocks, sausages and wine
brought from foreign lands.
Bring so much we'll have to stack the dishes,
and I'll empty every one, from wine to fowl to fishes.
Landlord, let your cares depart;
hasten, for your wine consoles a saddened heart.

All you bring must be well spiced,
more than merely what sufficed;
build in us a fire.
May fumes arise our drinks to meet
like the smoke from flaming heat;
cause us to perspire
so that we feel wetter than a mop.
Give our mouths the smell of an apothecary shop,
and, if wine should still my tongue,
landlord, pour down more until my song is sung.

Through me leads a busy road;
send along a heavy load,
food to make one gloat.
Wine enough to drive a mill
should rush beside the road, and will;
I must praise my throat.
I could take a goose to swallow whole.
Autumn, let me be your helper and your joys extoll.
On a roast my soul resides,
where it floats above the grapes' fermented tides.

The increasingly strong influence of the songs of the *Spielleute* on courtly verse is especially apparent in the twenty-two *Sprüche* which appear in a single manuscript under the pseudonym of Der Unverzagte (The Undaunted). We know little of the poet, not even the name, only that one of his songs places him in the second half of the century, another indicates that he was of noble birth, and others show that he was a wanderer who was dependent on his art for support. The language of his verses would identify him as being from Middle Germany, were it not for the fact that the scribe who recorded his work was from that area and may well have translated the singer's verses into his own dialect. Der Unverzagte composed neither erotic nor religious verse. He sings in a didactic, sometimes amusing vein of the duties and responsibilities of the rulers, of the virtues which young men should acquire, of the life of a wandering musician. With regard to form his verse is quite simple. He composed in three different *Töne*, the melodies of which have been preserved.

The 'good King Rudolph' of the first song was Rudolph I, a relatively obscure nobleman who founded the Hapsburg dynasty in Austria and was elected emperor of the Holy Roman Empire in 1273. It is hard to say to what extent the song was intended to be ironical, for Rudolph was actually a very enlightened ruler for his day; on the other hand, he was known for his parsimony. It will be noted that the poet mentions three different types of performance: singing, playing, and speaking. The 'speaking' performance probably refers to the recitation of long narrative

works such as *Tristan and Isolde*. In the second song Der Unver-
zagte lauds his profession and speaks of the singer's power, as the
journalist and historian of the period, to make or destroy the
reputations of princes and kings. In 'Learn Good Manners,
Youth of Twenty' the poet gives advice to young men. Many
of the courtly singers from Walther on felt a particular obligation
to instruct the youth, and since their audiences at court included
many young pages who were learning the duties and skills of a
knight, they had ample opportunity to do so. The last song is
one of the few which praises string music and honors the
instrumentalist as well as the vocalist. Although he reflects the
general opinion of the day in ranking song above strings, Der
Unverzagte was no doubt a fiddler as well as a singer. Most of
the composer-performers were. In his praise of the value of song
can be seen once again the singer's pride, not in his class, as was
the case with other aristocratic composers, but in his position
as a professional musician.

THE GOOD KING RUDOLPH LOVES HIS GOD

(Der kuninc rodolp mynnet got)

The good King Rudolph loves his God   and is a true believer,
the good King Rudolph has renounced   the evils which can
                                                        hurt you,
the good King Rudolph judges well,   abhoring each deceiver,
the good King Rudolph is indeed   a paragon of virtue,
the good King Rudolph honors God   and ladies that are
                                                        pretty,
the good King Rudolph oft is seen   performing acts of pity.
I grant him gladly all the grace   his charity may earn
who likes to hear the minstrels sing and fiddle and speak
                                    and gives them naught in turn.

WHOM WANDERING MINSTRELS VISIT

(Swen gerende liute gerne suochent)

Whom wandering minstrels visit has   esteem and reputation,
whom wandering minstrels shun has faults   which bring him
little fame,
whom wandering minstrels like to see,   he lives as fits his
station,
whom wandering minstrels would avoid   deserves contempt
and shame,
whom wandering minstrels love is one   on whom you can
depend,
whom wandering minstrels hate is false   and would not help
a friend,
whom wandering minstrels praise, beneath   a lucky star was
born,
whom wandering minstrels curse has lost   his honor and shall
reap disdain and scorn.

LEARN GOOD MANNERS, YOUTH OF TWENTY

(Junger man von tzwenzich iaren)

Learn good manners, youth of twenty,
virtue brings reward in plenty,
love the Lord unceasingly is my advice.
Then your hopes will not deceive you
and your virtue will not leave you,
but protect you from the evils that entice.
Here a robe of constancy and chasteness wear,
heaven then will send you pleasures.
Honor women all as treasures,
so will you receive an angel's garment there.

(Ez ist ein lobeliche kunst)

It is an art which all revere
to play well on a fiddle's strings;
the fiddler makes our spirits light,
but song shall have my praises here.
Song teaches women, men, and kings,
song makes God's table still more bright.
To song the sounds of strings belong,
who loves them more than minnesong
will have to do without my praises.
Song can be writ in words and phrases
to cure the world of its malaises.

MIDDLE CLASS COMPOSERS
OF COURTLY SONGS

During the course of the thirteenth century, while the courtly lyric was adopting new themes and attitudes, a new type of musician appeared in ever larger numbers: the professional middle class composer and performer of courtly songs. His appearance was a symptom of social, political, and economic changes which were taking place not only in the German-speaking lands, but throughout Western Europe. With the decline in the power of the Empire, which set in after the Hohenstaufen period, came a decrease in the importance of the emperor's chief allies, the minor nobility. This was accompanied by a decay of chivalric idealism, a lessening of class consciousness, and a gradual decline of the specifically aristocratic culture. At the same time, because trade and the guild system were replacing the feudal economy, the towns and their merchants and craftsmen were becoming increasingly important. The cultural center of gravity, which in the twelfth century had shifted from the monasteries to the courts, in the following century began to shift from the courts to the towns. Many citizens became literate and learned poetic and musical composition, perhaps from some impecunious aristocratic singer. These educated middle class composers were familiar with the works of their knightly predecessors and contemporaries and accepted in toto the traditions of courtly song. Indeed, it is often difficult or even impossible to ascertain definitely as to whether a particular composer was a nobleman or a citizen. However, when the latter produced chivalric songs he dealt with concepts and conceits that were foreign to his own life and heritage, and, therefore, was more mechanical and less convincing than his aristocratic colleague. Indeed, although he used the forms of the classical minnesong, the middle class composer was likely to treat mainly themes which were not specifically chivalric. He produced more religious and didactic songs than minnesongs, but did not to any significant extent deal with middle class life. The clear distinction between popular and courtly song was preserved; whether the middle class singer performed at the courts or in the towns, his art was aristocratic and quite different from the folksongs of the *Spielleute*.

Among the most interesting works by middle class singers are those of Master Alexander or, as one manuscript has it, 'The Wild Alexander.' He was a wanderer, probably a Swabian, and composed during the last quarter of the thirteenth century. This is as much biographical information as can be derived from his works. These consist of a Christmas song, a song of childhood, three minnesongs (one with a nature introduction), a *Minneleich*, and twenty-four *Spruch* stanzas in which he exhorts with the voice of an Old Testament prophet against the evils of a worldly life. The *Sprüche*, the *Leich*, and to a lesser extent the songs are characterized by darkness, an indefiniteness of expression, obscure symbolism, and allegory. The designation 'The Wild,' however, does not describe his utterence, but only refers to his wandering life. With one exception Alexander's *Töne* are quite simple.

The song, 'Long Ago as Boys Together,' begins as a simple and charming tale of childhood and, had the poet left it that way, would have been almost unique in Middle High German lyric verse. However, Alexander's penchant for allegorizing takes over in the middle of the song, to its detriment. The snake is, of course, that of the Garden of Eden, the pony represents Adam and with him all mankind, the foolish virgins are those of the New Testament parable. It has been suggested that the song was inspired by Vergil's third eclogue. In 'Oh, That One with Love Must Win,' the composer presents a minnesong which is traditional in language and spirit while being in one respect rather original: although not a dawn song, it describes both lovers as suffering from the pangs of love. But Alexander obviously was not deeply impressed by *minne*; he has little to say about its joys and is rather vague when, as in this poem, he sings of its sorrows. On the other hand, the simple structure lends itself to an immediacy of expression which makes the total effect both intimate and pleasing. Alexander's attitude toward chivalric love is more fully illustrated in his *Minneleich*, 'The Cause of My Despairing.' It announces the singer's dedication, not to the service of a particular woman, but to love itself. He anticipates no happiness in the service of love, but accepts it only as a sad duty. The preoccupation with the symbolism of the shield is characteristic of Alexander and suggests the Biblical allegories of the song of childhood and of the *Sprüche*.

LONG AGO AS BOYS TOGETHER

(Hie bevorn dô wir kynder waren)

Long ago as boys together
we would race in summer weather
free as any careless rover
through the blooming fields of clover,
and in calmer hours
gather flowers
where you see the cows and drover.

I remember, we were bending
down to pick the blooms, contending
which the fairest were, and we
wove us wreaths and danced with glee,
childish faces beaming,
flowers streaming,
in those times that used to be.

Seeking berries, we would wander
to the distant beeches yonder,
over stick and stone would run
till the setting of the sun,

till the forest ranger
(then no stranger)
said, 'Go home now. Day is done.'

Though we got a lot of scratches
racing through the berry patches,
that was sport, we did not care.
Shepherds told us to beware,
when they saw us playing,
always saying,
'Children, snakes are everywhere.'

Once a playmate, who was lying
in a thicket, rushed out crying,
'There's a snake! Where it is stony!
It's the one that bit our pony,
so that we can never
cure him ever.
He is still so sick and bony.'

Leave the forest and your playing,
go at once, without delaying,
or you'll suffer great distress.
If you linger, nonetheless,
in the forest vale,
you'll bewail
all your vanished happiness.

Once five foolish virgins tarried
when their ruler's son was married,
till at last he locked the hall
and ignored their fearful call
when the watchmen there
stripped them bare,
till they had no clothes at all.

(Ôwe daz nach liebe gât)

Oh, that one with love must win
always much of pain!
Love demands that I begin
verses in this vein.
She herself spoke thus to me:
'Tell of pain beyond all wonder
when two loves are torn asunder
sadly and eternally.'

Of me and my lady too
I well may tell such grief,
for when we pledge that we'll be true
we'll know, without relief,
naught but sorrow every day.
Love has power to enchant us
and for loyalty will grant us
little joy and great dismay.

For when we fell into Love's snare
then all our joys were dead,
but still we lived with heavy care
in sorrow and in dread.
Life is death for every lover;
Lady Love, restrain thy rages,
be more sparing with thy wages!
Let me die and her recover.

Just kill me now and let her live.
Spoke Love, 'It shall not be.
To them who wear my crest I give
both joy and misery.
I'd be false to name and art
and from duty would be turning,
should I not distress with yearning
two who are so far apart.'

For me a year would be a day,
if she were with me now,
and all my grief would pass away,
if fortune would allow
us such happiness and cheer.
But till then this pain I'll carry
even when my friends are merry,
and each day will be a year.

THE CAUSE OF MY DESPAIRING

(Myn trurichlichez klagen)

The cause of my despairing
is that I've lost my art
through my woe.
But must I go on, bearing
the sorrow in my heart,
ever so,
the burning torment fanned
by love's command?
 No, I must indeed from such a grief
find quick relief,
the breath
of death
drive away
or be a prey
every day
unceasingly to sorrow's sting.
Just as the swan
who knows anon
the hour when comes his death, as he I sing.
 O fruitful vine of all enjoyment,
O thou who gives my soul employment,
thou my loyal confidence,
my consolation and defence,
 ah, love, may I thy gifts esteem,

a stringent life, a precious dream!
Must I leave my lady fair
sword and shield for thee to bear?
    Well may he his fate bemoan
who must bear the shield alone.
That is need beyond all need
when a faithful knight takes up the shield
and leaves with passion unrevealed,
O, that's a living death indeed.
    So let the twain then come together,
they'll be so merry in any weather
that joy above all joy is born.
But sorrow later comes to wreck
their bliss and put them both in check,
parting leaves the pair forlorn,
    Love is the preserver
of him who wants to serve her
faithfully through thick and thin.
O, but sorrow is her twin!
    Who her shield would carry
now is sad, now merry.
He must suffer joy and pain
just as love may so ordain.
    We were told
by the old
of desire and dread,
of the many who sped
to the realm of the dead,
struck down by passion's mighty blow.
Inform me,
thou stormy
love, how I may praise
thee and all they ways
well with pretty lays,
that all thy friends may know.
    And praised be he
who is free
but desires to be the thane

of courtly love for high rewards.
I shall now
tell him how
he may gain, and entertain
with words of love and sweetest chords.
　　Now listen, thus the shield is made,
beneath it many bards have played,
a naked child on field of red
with sightless eyes and jewelled head,
a golden arrow in one hand,
the other holds a flaming brand.
　　And, toward the edges, stretching wide,
its wings are spread in hurried flight,
the shield is decked on either side
with coat of arms and colors bright.
　　Do you know her fame
and how she came
to us in word and body, too?
The infant there
cannot compare,
the glosses say that this is true.
Love, awaken,
firm, unshaken,
work, that all the mighty throng
thee may claim,
with dart and flame
and let us see who then is strong!
　　And truly, here comes Cupid flying,
torch and bow and arrow plying.
His arrow pierces all attire
and then you, too, shall spread the fire.
A burning flame of joy and zest
has entered Cupid's seething breast.
　　Though he storms and rages wildly,
this is but a youthful sport,
thus one pictures him so childly.
He knows tricks of every sort.
　　He wears the crown

with a stately frown
who met and conquered many a king.
Give way, give way,
how strong his sway!
He overcomes each mortal thing.
  Sees and kisses
pretty misses,
goes, but soon appears again.
If he chances
on loving glances,
O, he sends his arrow then.
  Pity, Cupid, pity,
spare the young and pretty.
One small dart comes flying,
two with love are sighing,
ensnared by thee completely,
just for smiling sweetly.
  Thou art in their land,
rage not with thy brand.
When breast to breast comes nigher
then kindles with desire
a flame upon the street,
thou burnest with great heat.
  I regret thy blindness greatly,
for when cowards love too lately
then must Cupid act, and straightly.
Your game was ever blind and bare,
let others tell it if they care,
I'll say no more of this affair.
  Wishing and dreaming
float as a feather,
thou guidest with scheming
high and nether,
thy darts, brightly gleaming,
speed quickly and bring all lovers together.
  Shield, relate thy story.
Thy field is red,
man for woman's glory

to pain is led,
the one is bruised and gory,
the other one is cold and dead.
Who the shield would carry
always must be merry,
although the infant strong
orders him to follow long
the song
which Paris brought us over sea,
stolen from the Spartan,
the love-sick swain to hearten.
Since the Greeks regained their prize,
who is fettered by love's ties
now cries
nothing but 'Alas! Ah me!'

Alexander was proud of his profession and very conscious of his responsibility as a poet with regard to the morality of his listeners. Although this pride and the accompanying sense of responsibility can be seen throughout the history of the courtly song, it is most apparent in the works of its middle class composers. One who was especially aware of his duties to society and to history was Robyn. There were apparently two singers with the name Robyn or Rubin. One was a Tyrolean nobleman, a contemporary of Walther von der Vogelweide, the other was a commoner who lived one or two generations later. The *Spruch* below is one of two composed by the latter, a singer of whom nothing more is known than that he probably grew up in central Germany.

ONE DARE NOT GREET WITH PRAISES

(Nie man tzu vrô sol prŷsen)

'One dare not greet with praises
too soon the breaking day.'
thus spoke the ancient sages

long ago and plainly.
Splendidly may glow the morning
which later turns to gray,
perhaps with little warning,
and praise was given vainly.
Let singers then move slowly,
that honor be rightly meted,
to know the great men wholly
before their deeds are feted.
Praise won by actions lowly
is infamy repeated.

The most productive and one of the two most famous of the middle-class singers who composed in the courtly tradition was Konrad von Würzburg. He was born between 1220 and 1230 in the city of Würzburg where he apparently also spent his youth and received a good education, not only in the German and Latin literature of his day and in classical literature, but also in theological and legal matters. While still a young man, he moved to Strassburg and then to Basle, where he settled permanently. He died in 1287 and was buried in the cathedral there.

Konrad was the first German poet-musician to support himself as an independent professional artist through performances and commissions. His patrons and clients were not nobles, but middle-class patricians and wealthy clergymen. He was very popular among his contemporaries, as is indicated by the large number of manuscripts of his works, and exerted a strong influence on his successors down into the fifteenth century. Rumesland and Hermann Damen praised and imitated him, Frauenlob composed a eulogy at his death, and the sixteenth century Master Singers adopted him as one of the Twelve Great Masters. This popularity was due, at least in part, to Konrad's versatility and productivity. In all, he composed some 58,000 lines of verse dealing with religious and secular material in epic and lyric form. He treated German and classical legends and sagas, and historical and contemporary themes. One of his longer works dealt with the Lohengrin story, another with the Trojan War.

His lyric works include nine summer songs, eleven winter songs, two dawn songs, a religious *Leich*, a dance *Leich*, and forty-four *Sprüche*, dealing chiefly with religious and political matters.

In his songs Konrad shows himself to be a master of language and a virtuoso of style who, as a technician, is unmatched in German literature. He was adept at coining words and obtaining variety of expression through synonyms. He employed alliteration and an astonishing wealth of rhyme in his ceaseless search for originality of style and refinement of technique. Indeed, he often develops a highly complex pattern of initial, interior, and end rhyme which is quite impossible to translate. In one song every syllable, unstressed as well as stressed, in a line rhymes with the corresponding syllable in another line, producing a symmetrical pattern in which every syllable in the poem bears a rhyme. And yet, despite this *tour de force*, nothing is strained or awkward. However, for all of his versatility and virtuosity, Konrad does not rank with the best of the courtly composers; he was a master craftsman, but not a great artist.

Although Konrad composed in the general courtly tradition, his works contain many non-courtly elements. One such was a baroque affinity for the ugly and grotesque, as is evident in the song, 'When I Begin to Drowse, I Feel as if My Life Were Done.' Also the treatment here of the transitory nature of life and the omnipresence of death, though favorite themes of Middle Latin verse, is somewhat foreign to both the courtly song and the courtly *Weltanschauung*. The following song, 'May with Wondrous Skill,' is closer to the traditional minnesong, but an adaptation to a bourgeois audience is apparent even here. For the praise of springtime does not merely serve as an introduction to the subject, it is the subject, and in the quite secondary treatment of love there is no indication that either the narrator or his listeners are of the nobility.

(Mir ist als ich niht lebende sî)

When I begin to drowse, I feel   as if my life were done
and sleep becomes a symbol of   the death which I would shun.
With the setting sun
my shadow always teaches me
that life, like it, must fade;   and I'm reminded of the heat
of hell whenever in   the bathing house I take a seat.
Flowers tell how fleet
the gleam of transient joy can be.
In the mirror I can see   that I to dust must go,
and the charnel houses show
with their bones and smell
that worms will feed with unclean mouths   upon this mortal
shell.
If I do not abstain from sin,   then I shall later dwell
in the depths of hell
and suffer there eternally.

MAY WITH WONDROUS SKILL

(Manger wunne bilde)

May with wondrous skill
in idle hours
created lovely things.
See, to vale and hill,
bedecked with flowers,
such a silken shimmer clings.
Trees put on their clothes, behold
their crowns of leafy splendor!
Bird song, clear and tender:
a manifold
choir of forest voices sings.
Summer tide

doth provide
all the world with ecstasy.
What a wealth of joy has he
whose love is by his side.

May stills grief and pain,
and rich rewards
it bestows on hill and dale.
From the blooms a strain
of sweetest chords
comes from many a nightingale.
Violets blue and clover green
and daffodils of gold,
roses red unfold,
the fairest are seen
everywhere in wood and swale.
Summer tide
doth provide
all the world with ecstasy.
What a wealth of joy has he
whose love is by his side.

He, who at this time
doth love a maid,
and through such delights can stroll,
with a joy sublime
shall be repaid.
Love makes wounded hearts now whole.
Beauty for his eye appears
which apple blossoms bring,
and the birds all sing
to charm his ears.
Then shall love rejoice his soul.
Summer tide
shall provide
all the world with ecstasy.
What a wealth of joy has he
whose love is by his side.

Hermann Damen, one of the composers who was especially influenced by Konrad von Würzburg, was the son of a respected citizen of the North German city of Rostock. He composed during the last quarter of the thirteenth century and the first decade of the fourteenth century; one *Leich* and a number of shorter works, mainly *Sprüche*, are extant. Damen's compositions do not differ greatly from those of the other middle-class singers of his time. His work is chiefly of a didactic and religious nature and his style is characterized by an occasional *tour de force* of rhyme.

The simplicity of form of the song, 'Would the World but Show Me Kindness,' offers a pleasant contrast to Damen's usual, rather ornate style. The unrhymed line, called an 'orphan,' was borrowed by the early minnesingers from Provençal song. Five other *Sprüche* dealing with similar themes were written in the same *Ton*. The song, 'To Grace This Melody I Brought,' illustrates in two ways the decadence of the late courtly song. In the first place, it shows art turned in upon itself: it is a poem about poetry. In the second place, the use of rhyme is highly pretentious (every tenth line rhymes), revealing the skill of the poet probably without contributing anything to the ear of the listener. Although it is possible that the medieval audience had a more retentive memory for such things than does a modern. The first line of the song is interesting in that it adds evidence to the theory that the minnesingers were more likely to put words to tunes than the reverse. Damen's pleasure in the manipulation of rhyme is especially noticeable in 'I Shall Sing Thy Love Excelling.' In addition to thrice repeated end rhyme, he adds, in the fourteenth and final lines, initial rhyme. Damen liked this *Ton* and composed nine *Sprüche* to it. The last song, 'The Master of the Marvelous,' is simple in form and direct in expression. It shows the poet at his best: singing in a rather prosaic, but sincere manner of elementary Christian teachings.

(Het ich al der werlde hulde)

Would the world but show me kindness,
then what joy would I possess.
God forgive them for their blindness
who would steal my happiness.
I know such knaves, and do not love them,
those who envy all good people
and can say but evil of them.

TO GRACE THIS MELODY I BROUGHT

(Ich mâle of des sanges syms)

To grace this melody I brought
the fairest words I could devise,
but you must help to brighten
gloomy darkness in my verse.
You thus shall give me aid
and earn the other poets' praise.
So weave with thought the charm of verse
within your heart
and they'll commend you greatly.
I shall also honor you,
for I am heartily afraid that ever
my art may weigh still less than thought
when measured with another's prize.
The judging scales will heighten
the fame of one, condemn the worse
and show us where was made
an error or an awkward phrase,
that one may see and form a perfect work of art,
whose words are blended stately
with the tune and meter too.
The song shall then bring praises for endeavor.
It honors man, exalts the wives,
gives wisdom for tomorrow.

The singer can
give many lives
relief from pain and sorrow.
For song the splendor of art has wrought,
and he who masters song shall rise
to fame, and praise shall lighten
his heart, and all his cares disperse.
In this my hopes are laid,
that I may rightly form my lays.
Whoever wears the crown of song and will
impart
its verse and tune sedately,
singing nothing he may rue,
shall wear it long and find it weighty never.

I SHALL SING THY LOVE EXCELLING

(Eyn lob syng ich dir tzu prîse)

I shall sing Thy love excelling,
in my song Thy praises telling,
so that I may share Thy dwelling
when life has its ending.
Never shall his guile disarm me,
who would lie in wait to harm me,
neither shall his hate alarm me
with my Lord defending.
I shall not be his prey,
my allegiance he shall never gain,
and he shall have no pay
for his toil but everlasting pain.
Thou Three-In-One, transcending,
sending   down the word that frees us,
from the evil which would seize us,
through the love that seeks to please us,
Jesus,   save unending.

(Der aller wunder meister ist)

The master of the marvelous
who made each earthly creature,
this truly is the Christ, to us
friend and teacher
who died for everyone.
Of all that hovers in the air,
of all the ocean's treasure,
to man is given that most fair
for his pleasure
through the gift of God's own Son.
Were there not compassion
in the power of His arm,
there would be no refuge
to save the poor from harm.
His bounteous mercy can erase
all of our transgression,
to him who seeks a resting place
and intercession
He will grant His saving grace.

A pupil of Hermann Damen was Heinrich von Meissen, better
known as Frauenlob. The latter was born about 1260, probably
in or near the city of Meissen, of peasant or middle-class parents.
He attained local distinction as a singer and composer at an
early age and left home when about fifteen to begin his career.
He travelled first to the south. In 1278 he was with the army of
King Rudolph of Austria and was the chief performer at a large
festival during which the king knighted the young squires who
had been serving at his court. In 1292 Frauenlob was in Bo-
hemia and sang on the occasion of the knighting of King Wenzel
II. A few years later he was in Carinthia, the southeastern part
of present-day Austria. His wanderings then took him to the
north, to Brandenburg, Mecklenburg, Bremen, and Denmark.
In these states he sang at various important festivals and was

treated more as an honored guest than as an entertainer. About 1312 he went to the city of Mainz as the most famous minnesinger of his day and remained there, probably under the sponsorship of Archbishop Peter von Aspelt, until his death. Legend, supported by an engraving on his tombstone, says that Frauenlob's casket was carried to its resting place by eight beautiful girls. He is buried at the Cathedral of Mainz, but the exact spot is no longer known.

The most characteristic features of Frauenlob's art are the result of his philosophic and pietiestic inclinations. He was familiar with the principal tenets of scholasticism, which saw the moral and physical world as a uniform representation of divine wisdom. The omnipresence of divine reason became the central factor in Frauenlob's thinking and therefore the traditional words and concepts of chivalry, as he uses them, have new meanings and values. His concept of *minne* is different from that of his predecessors and becomes a rather abstract virtue. Sometimes it means married love, a divine necessity for society; sometimes it has spiritual significance, becoming a love of divinity or a guide to knowledge of divinity.

Frauenlob composed three *Leiche*, thirteen minnesongs, and about 450 stanzas of *Sprüche*, the latter in fifteen different *Töne*. His verse is characterized by a lively fantasy; by a baroque playing with words, pictures, and parables; and by vague, not readily comprehensible concepts. His similes and metaphors, when not biblical, are more often drawn from middle-class life than from that of the nobility. The Master Singers mistakenly celebrated Frauenlob as the founder of the first of their singing schools.

Most of Frauenlob's *Sprüche* appear in groups of three, which can be presented as three-stanza songs. The *Sprüche* which are introduced by the line, 'My joys, alas, have vanished,' were probably composed shortly before the minnesinger's death. Indeed, he may have known at the time of composition that he was dying. This song must have been quite popular, for it appears in five different sources. In the *Spruch* which begins, 'I hear my father's proverb say,' Frauenlob gives advice to the rulers of the German states; however, unlike Walther von der

Vogelweide, he does not advocate specific courses of action, but confines himself to general matters of policy and behavior. His tendency to use words in a broadly symbolic manner is illustrated in this *Spruch* by the reference to the 'door' and the 'flood of life.' The stanzas which begin with 'Lo, I saw a maiden' are the first two segments of Frauenlob's most famous work, 'The Lay of Our Lady.' The first segment forms a song which in its simplicity of structure and content resembles the folksong. The second segment is complex in structure and its language is rather symbolic and abstract. It consists of two stanzas in which rhyme within the individual stanzas appears and also rhyme between corresponding lines of both stanzas. In the latter case the rhyme words are ten lines apart. The question once more arises as to whether such rhyming was merely a game which the author played for his own amusement or was actually an effective poetic device. It was doubtless from this Marian *Leich* that Frauenlob received his pseudonym, which means 'praise of the lady.'

MY JOYS, ALAS, HAVE VANISHED

(Mŷn vroud ist gar czugangyn)

My joys, alas, have vanished,   now hear this sorrowful lament:
I rue the sore offenses   with which my days on earth were spent.
Often have I gone astray,
now death will take me and the world forget me.
My life will soon be over,   since death my early end has sworn;
whatever gifts I offer,   all are lost and I must mourn,
for he will summon me away;
alas, the haunting fears that now beset me!
No cheerful heart can save me,
nor wisdom, nor can haughtiness,   nor love the ladies gave me.
My virtue, strength, endeavor:
all are lost and I must mourn.
Who chose my company forlorn
is fearful death; with him I leave forever.

Now death would tear asunder   my life and me, and thus am I
so overcome with sorrow.   Oh God, in mercy hear my cry.
Receive my soul, my body may
again to earth and to the worms be given.
My art, my poet's spirit   will fade within my heart's confine;
Oh, who may these inherit,   for they can be no longer mine,
God giveth and He takes away;
may I receive the joys for which I've striven!
My songs I'll sing no longer,
now hear these words of deep distress,   death waxes ever
                                             stronger,
now heed my warning surely:
I speak to men and ladies all,
since each a prey to death must fall,
to righteousness hold fast and keep securely.

Maria, spotless mother,   because of they beloved Son
remember me in mercy.   And Thou, whose pain redemption
                                             won
on the cross where all might view
the bloody spear which pierced Thy side, O Savior.
It was a Jew who thrust it,   but Thou forgave his wicked deed,
and so I pray Thee, Master,   because of Thy distress and need
when Thou wert wounded by the Jew,
because of all Thy pain show me Thy favor.
Oh weep, ye eyes once merry!
Sir Death, what canst thou want with me?   My tears will help
                                             to bury
poor Frauenlob in flowing,
for bitter death my end hath willed.
Oh God, why must this voice be stilled?
So let it be, and few will mark my going.

(Ich hore des vater lêre ihen)

I hear my father's proverb say, 'Child, if you would see
value in yourself, then let this be.
The less of grief, the more of fear;
keep within your heart the words which now you hear,
thus you can seek the counsel that you need.'
You princes must be cautious, too;
who comes to you
not by the door, his counsel is not true.
Have both your thumbs right in your hands;
be careful whom you trust with honor, power, and lands.
I see straight through
the honied stratagems and greed.
One marks how often fortune's stay is brief,
how bliss can change to pain without relief
and joy can end in grief.
These truths, you princes, recognize,
if you'd be wise
and would arise
the flood of life to lead.

LO, I SAW A MAIDEN

(Ey ich sach in dem trône)

Lo, I saw a maiden
with child upon a throne,
her crown was heavy laden
with many a precious stone.
She wished to be delivered,
the best of maidens said;
a dozen diamonds quivered
and sparkled on her head.
  When nature's course was run,
the lovely one
brought forth a child, a wondrous son,
in labor, as another.
Her wisdom first could see
that he
with seven lamps was there.
She saw him then arise
a lamb before her view
on Zion's mountain peak.
  She did all that she could,
the sweet and good,
and bore the flower of field and wood.
If you became the mother
of lamb or peaceful dove
of love,
oh maidens, you would swear
('t would be no great surprise)
her food would bring to you
the fruit for which you seek.

12

INDIAN SUMMER

In comparison with the two preceding centuries the fourteenth century was throughout most of its extent quite barren of lyric production, for from Frauenlob and Wizlaw, who were still composing at the beginning of the century, until its last two decades no important poet appeared. From about 1380 to 1420, however, some two hundred years after the golden age of Middle High German, there was a renaissance of song which produced a great deal of significant poetry and music. This Indian summer occurred in the south and centers primarily around three poet-composers—Hugo von Montfort, Hermann the Monk of Salzburg, and Oswald von Wolkenstein—who together composed some 266 poems and a large number of melodies.

The oldest of the three poets, Count Hugo VIII of Montfort-Bregenz and Tannenberg, was a highly respected and influencial nobleman with extensive estates scattered through Austria. He was born in the year 1357 in the Vorarlberg region near the present borders of Germany and Switzerland. As a boy he was a page at the Viennese court where, in addition to learning the manners and duties of a knight, he was instructed in the art of poetic composition. At the age of sixteen he entered into the first of three apparently happy and certainly very profitable marriages. In later years he distinguished himself as a soldier in a crusade against the heathen Prussians, in a campaign in Italy, and in various engagements in defense of his outlying estates against Swiss and Bohemian encroachments. In the service of Duke Leopold III of Hapsburg he proved himself to be an able diplomat and statesman, for which he received many honors. He died in 1423.

Forty poems appear in manuscripts under Montfort's name, but the authenticity of two has been questioned. His compositions include *Sprüche*, minnesongs, and letters in verse. Montfort breathed new life and vigor into the minnesong, or, one might say, he changed it into something different and more modern. His earliest songs are conventional, but, as a mature artist, he produced contemporary works which reflected personal feelings and experiences, revealed the manners and mores of his own time, and had little to do with outworn traditions. Although clearly the work of an intelligent and educated man, they stand closer to the folksongs of his day than to the classical minnesong. They were composed in the few leisure hours of a busy life, some of them on horseback as Montfort rode from one to another of his estates.

Montfort did not compose his own melodies, but depended for them on a vassal, Burk Mangolt. It was probably not unusual for a minnesinger, particularly one who was a wealthy nobleman, to employ a composer for his songs; however, that he should freely admit this and give due credit to the composer is unique in the history of medieval song and speaks much for Montfort's honesty.

Montfort, like Wolfram, was partial to the dawn song and composed quite a number of them. The first selection below is one of his earliest dawn songs and is fairly traditional in content except that the relationship between the two lovers is proper. The simplicity of Montfort's metrics here offers a welcome relief from the virtuosity of his immediate predecessors and gives the song a more personal flavor. The following selection, 'At Dawn a Watchman Was Scolding Me,' illustrates the poet's tendency to change the traditional forms of the minnesong. Although it contains the person of the watchman and is written as a dialogue, it is not a dawn song in the usual sense, for it has nothing to do with the parting of lovers. It also breaks with tradition in that it does not sing the praises of a particular lady-love, but is a eulogy of all women, both wives and sweethearts. The presence of unrhymed lines shows the influence of the *Spielmann* song. In the third song, 'Tell Me, Watchman, of the Morn,' he again uses the form of the dawn song for new subject matter, a description of the wonder of creation. The poem has three stanzas, but parts of the final two are missing in the manuscript. The positions of the unrhymed lines have caused the question to be raised in this case as to whether the song was altered in transmission. It could be possible, for Montfort spoke a different dialect from that in which the manuscript is written. However, since he himself said that he was a poor rhymer, it should be assumed that the lines were originally unrhymed. The stanza entitled 'Dame World, You Are so Sweet and Fair,' is the first stanza of a long poem composed, as subsequent verses indicate, at the time of the death of Montfort's second wife, in 1401. It is an alternating song in which the singer declares his intention of renouncing worldly pleasures and Dame World attempts to dissuade him. Each stanza is divided equally between the two antagonists. Such arguments between a man on the one hand and Dame World, Lady Venus, or a pagan spirit on the other were popular throughout the medieval period and also appeared in the folk ballads of later times. One of the latter was adapted by Goethe for his famous 'Erlkönig.' Montfort's description of Dame World as a beautiful woman who leads men to destruction closely resembles that of Dame Venus in 'The Ballad of Tannhäuser.' The last selection, 'Wake, Awaken, Lovely Sleeper,' is the first stanza of a four-stanza song which was composed in praise of the poet's third wife. Montfort's independence of tradition is seen in his use of a dawn song, which ordinarily tells only of stolen love, to present a warm and personal testimony to his marital happiness.

AT EVENING I AWAIT ALONE

(Ich frow mich gen des âbentz kunft)

At evening I await alone
the night, when she will come to me,
and so will make her favor known;
my hopes are high as they can be
that she her kindness will reveal.

Had I no pleasure in such charm,
I'd be a man of brass or steel.

The church bell brings us sweet distress
and then I hear the watchman's horn;
we share a kiss, a fond caress,
for we must part with breaking morn.
Such parting is a grievance sore,
but, if I thought I'd not return,
then I would sorrow even more.

With us decorum must prevail
and modesty our love restrain,
should someone tell another tale,
then would it cause us woe and pain.
Now Jupiter and Venus pale,
they flee before the rising sun,
the day has come to wood and dale.

AT DAWN A WATCHMAN WAS SCOLDING ME

(Mich strâft ain wachter des morgens frü)

At dawn a watchman was scolding me:
'When will you ever rest,' said he,
'and let this singing end?
Write no more songs upon your scroll,
is my advice upon my soul,
to which the people dance.'
'Watchman, your words I'll not ignore,
such dancing songs I'll write no more,
of this you may be sure.
But lovely wives I still must praise,
they brighten life's distressing days,
My God, how dear they are!
And he who ill of them has sung,
were I to say, should lose his tongue,
he would deserve such shame.

'Watchman, now mark and judge their worth,
whatever I have seen on earth
is but an idle breeze
compared to the love of wife or maid,
here neither art nor sense can aid,
and this was always true.
David, even Solomon,
Sampson, too, was once undone,
he lost his life complete.
Therein did women have a part,
a virgin broke the seal of art.
Away, you ladies sweet!
Whoever women shall offend
will come to no congenial end.
They like not scorn or blame.

'Watchman, look at the firmament,
the day comes from the orient,
I hear the song of birds.
All blessed women may it wake,
may God protect them for His sake
from every traitor's tongue.
Who loves and tells is most unkind
and, though with seeing eyes, is blind,
he can't endure for long.
The roses all that I have seen,
the blossoms, all the foliage green
are but a jest to me
compared with lovely maidens' charm
with graceful bearing, glances warm,
God grant them blissful days.'

TELL ME, WATCHMAN, OF THE MORN

(Sag an wachter wie was es tag)

Tell me, watchman, of the morn
before the earth and sky were born,

226

before there were the elements and planets,
Then neither sun nor man made light,
but God in majesty and might
was there, who has no end and no beginning.
The word is God, and God the word;
all things were made when it was heard
and all were fair according to their nature.

DAME WORLD, YOU ARE SO SWEET AND FAIR

(Frô welt ir sint gar hüpsch und schön)

'Dame World, you are so sweet and fair,
but your reward's destruction.
Your loving words and lilting air
are magic of seduction.
Whoe'er devotes himself to you
is soon misled and straying
and at his end has much to rue.
I've often heard this saying.'
'Dearest companion, why this blame?
I gave thee courage, gave thee graces,
and yet must reap reproach and shame.
Come, learn of joy in my embraces,
leave care to the birds and live with me
and merrily dance each night instead
(with this advice I counsel thee),
a crown of roses on thy head.'

WAKE, AWAKEN, LOVELY SLEEPER

(Weka wekh die zarten lieben)

Wake, awaken, lovely sleeper!
I think it not unrightly done,
I wish not to deceive her,
the day begins to dawn.
In truth, she lingers never,

the waker of my heart's desire,
⁻her pleasure waxes ever
in service of her God.
Whoever has a loyal wife,
he has a treasure-trove of bliss.
Her praise and honor cheer his life.
I hear the song of birds,
I watch the starlight leave us,
I feel the cool of early morn,
but find that not so grievous.
Her face makes all so fair.

Although nearly 100 songs appear in some 50 different manuscripts under the name of The Monk of Salzburg, his identity has not been definitely established. It is most plausible to assume that he was a Prior Hermann who was perhaps ten years younger than Hugo von Montfort and whom records of the early fifteenth century connect to the Benedictine monastery in Salzburg. In any case the composer of the songs was a member of the circle of poets and musicians which gathered at the court of Archbishop Pilgrim II von Puchheim (1365-1396) in Salzburg. Over 40 of his religious songs and nearly 60 of his secular songs are extant. The former are largely adaptations of Latin hymns, the latter are for the most part in the courtly minnesong tradition, but some show a definite affinity to the folksong.

Unlike Montfort, The Monk was a master technician and his courtly minnesongs are characterized by a baroque playing with form and by highly complicated structural patterns and rhyme schemes. However, The Monk was as much inclined as the older poet to adapt chivalric concepts and content to his own time. He seldom makes a distinction between 'woman' and 'lady' and he was especially well known for his (uncourtly) harvest songs. In these he describes the St. Martin festivals in language much like that of Neidhart. Also like Neidhart are his descriptions of the physical charms of his beloved one. The fact that The Monk comes at the end of a tradition is seen particularly in the fact that in addition to minnesongs which do not differ greatly from those of the twelfth century he composed poly-phonic love songs, which really belong to modern rather than medieval times. Most of the melodies to The Monk's songs have been preserved. A reference in one of the manuscripts to a lay priest by the name of Martin who helped him with the songs has raised the possibility that Hermann, like Montfort, may not have composed the music to his songs.

The song, 'From Deep and Gentle Sleep,' presents adequate evidence of Hermann's technical skill, indeed, though it is not without poetic feeling, it gives something of the impression of a rhyming crossword puzzle. Caught up in the *tour de force* of rhyme, one can easily forget the girl of whom The Monk is singing. The lack of rhyme in the last line creates an effective element of surprise. The following song takes the traditional form of the love letter or *salut*. There are several other stanzas in addition to the one given, the last of which supplies the date, 1392, and identifies the sender of the letter as 'Pilgrim.' Although this certainly refers to Archbishop Pilgrim, it does not mean that he composed the song. The name of the town, Freudensal, means 'Hall of Joy' and was probably inspired by Neidhart's castle of Reuenthal (Valley of Regret). In 'O Lady, Dearest to My Sight' can be seen the two chief tendencies of the courtly song in the fifteenth century: toward the sterile and mechanical craftsmanship of the mastersong on the one hand and the sim-plicity of the folksong on the other. The first two lines with their regular tetrameter could have introduced a folksong, but then enjambement and parenthesis produce lines like those of a mastersong. One of Hermann's polyphonic works is 'Listen, Dearest Lady, to My Plight.' In this composition the traditional alternating song has become a dialogue which is accompanied by the continuous song of the watchman. The result might be called a secular motet. It is essentially a musical, rather than a poetic work, indeed, the directions on the manuscript suggest that a trumpet may be substituted for the lovers' dialogue.

FROM DEEP AND GENTLE SLEEP

(Gar lŷs, in senfter wŷs)

From deep
and gentle sleep,
my love, arise
and turn your eyes
to skies
where starlight flies
and darkly lies
the heaven's blue.
Awake, my charming maid, that you
in passion sweet
may greet
your heart, which dwells in me.
Your voice will be
a melody
to me
and thrill
me, if you will
but wish a fond 'Good day.'
Your glances say,
with many a gleaming
love-light beaming,
that your affections I possess.
My heart then leaps with happiness
and hope that my reward is near,
your eyes have promised me, my dear,
till it appear,
may I receive a greeting from your lips.

TO THE FAIREST, SWEETEST, ONE WHO LIVES

(Dem allerlibsten, schönsten weib)

To the fairest, sweetest one who lives
in Freudensal, Dame Honor Bright,
I send this little note, which gives

the best regards that I can write.
Source of all the joys I've sought,
know this: my heart and every thought
are sore distraught,
my days are long and bring me naught.
No one on earth is half so fine,
I like each way and worth of thine:
the path of honor thou didst choose,
such was thy nature and design.
No woman would I rather see.

O LADY, DEAREST TO MY SIGHT

(Zart libste frau in liber acht)

O lady, dearest to my sight,
wish me a pleasant, joyous night,
thy loyalty gives such delight
and ever leads my steps aright
when I'm away,
as now, that they
not stray.
I'm all alone
with none my own
to comfort me
but thee.
My longing drives away all sleep,
and see:
the whole night long for thee
I weep.
Sweet dreams such happiness supply
and always make me wish that I,
waking never,
might sleep forever
with pleasant dreams that never end.

(Hör, libste frau, mich deinen knecht)

[the lovers]
Listen, dearest lady, to my plight.
—What is all this long harangue at night?
—I only wish you, lady, well.
—Speak, what do you have to tell?
—What my longing heart befell.
—This desire that you pursue...
—Is, my dear, to be with you.
—Do not sorrow,
come tomorrow.
—Lady, stay!
—Why not come to me by day?
—What will evil gossips say?
—Nights they're watching all around.
—I stole here without a sound.
—Whisper low
what I'm to know.
—Joy and grief have filled my heart.
—Can't you tell the two apart?
—Grief is pain, but joy is nice.
—I can give you good advice.
—Do so, lady, counsel me.
—You must practice loyalty.

[the watchman]
I warn you both to flee,
honestly,
as I should,
for I only want your mutual good.
Who has honor, he has care,
I advise you to beware,
bliss the gossips cannot bear.
This is what I warn you of,
for when love is seeking love

it must fear their spite,
for their evil words can bite
as do deadly snakes.
See what pride the poisonous gossip takes
in his evil ways:
he brays
like an ass
of the honor of his class,
he'll surpass
all in boorish brass,
for he wants the rest to be
just as mean and low as he.
He indeed
swaggers when his wiles succeed.

Oswald von Wolkenstein, the last important Middle High German poet, was one of the most dynamic, colorful, and ruthless figures in the history of literature and music. He was born in 1377 as the second son of a wealthy and powerful knight of the southern Tirol. His life of adventure began at the age of ten when in the service of a German knight he left home on prolonged wanderings throughout the Near East and the lands surrounding the Mediterranean. He was absent for about thirteen years, during which time he learned, as one of his songs relates, ten languages. When his father died, Wolkenstein returned home to share the inheritance with his two brothers. Since all three were of a headstrong and avaricious nature, the sharing was accomplished only after some theft, violence, and even bloodshed; however, the brothers were not permanently estranged from one another.

A second, but shorter, period of wandering began for Wolkenstein in 1415 when he entered the service of King Sigmund of Hungary. At this time he travelled first to Spain and Portugal, where he took part in a battle, later to France and Italy, and finally to England and Scotland. In 1417 he returned home and was thereafter only infrequently absent from his homeland. This does not mean, however, that he settled down to a life of quiet domesticity. For after a year the poet took part in an unsuccessful revolt against Duke Friedrich of Austria and soon after the conclusion of these hostilities a property dispute which he had carried on for years with another noble family became violent. In 1421 Wolkenstein was lured into the hands of his enemies by a woman and was imprisoned. Eventually Duke Friedrich intervened in the dispute, but was not able to arrange any settlement; Wolkenstein, however, was set free. Six years later he was imprisoned again, this time by the Duke, and a final settlement of the property dispute was made. The settlement was not unfavorable to the poet, although he seems to have had no legitimate claim to the property he had seized. In his later years he became more and more influential in Tyrolean affairs, but he remained quite ruthless in his attempts to increase his holdings at the expense of others and without recourse to law. He was still vigorous and ambitious at his death in 1445.

Since the chief manuscripts which contain Wolkenstein's songs were prepared under his personal supervision, it is probable that all or nearly all of his compositions have been preserved. They comprise 127 poems, some quite long, and 124 melodies. The poems consist mainly of love songs, autobiographical songs, and moral or religious songs, however, there are also verses about hunting and drinking and some in which he pokes fun at the peasants in the manner of Neidhart. His dawn songs are particularly interesting for their wealth of detailed nature description. The poet's compositions are chiefly characterized by the strong impression of immediate experience which they give. His love songs have little to do with the courtly concept of *minne* and are openly sensual. One feels that they tell of real women whom the singer knew and of actual relationships with them. The autobiographical songs, too, have an unmistakable aura of authenticity and are commonly accepted as factual. The moral and religious verse, which was perhaps composed during Wolkenstein's imprisonments, also reveal a background of experience, but the sentiments expressed in them are rather formal and shallow in comparison with his other works. Most of the religious verse consists of Marian songs.

A second and equally important characteristic of the songs of

Wolkenstein's early and middle life is the remarkable unity which they achieve. In his best works melody, verse structure, rhythm, language, and content are adapted to each other with astonishing success. However, his compositions show a wide range of merit, and the poorer ones have little but technical proficiency to recommend them. It is only a short step from the later works of Wolkenstein to the uninspired and mechanical productions of the master singers.

The first selection below, 'Departed Is My Bosom's Woe,' is the first stanza and the refrain of a spring song. The stanza gives the words of the narrator, the refrain is sung by two birds in turn. The Mosmair who is mentioned was a farmer friend of Wolkenstein, the Isack is a river which flows by Hauenstein, the other proper nouns are place names. The song was probably composed between 1417 and 1421. The following selection is autobiographical. It deals with an action during the revolt of the Tyrolean nobles against Duke Friedrich II in the year 1418. These are the initial stanzas of a victory song which celebrates the successful defense of Greifenstein Castle against the troops of the duke. The word 'loan' in the third stanza also means the granting of a fief, so that the line has a double meaning, the second being that the singer is renouncing his feudal obligations to Friedrich. The lack of consistency of metrical structure which one sees in the stanzas is not infrequent with Wolkenstein. The dawn song, 'O Tell Me, Love, What Does It Mean,' is sung by a man, a woman, and the watchman's horn. The first two lines of the first two stanzas are sung by the woman, the final lines of the first two stanzas and the entire third stanza are sung by the horn. All three stanzas are in the discantus. The last three stanzas are sung by the man and are in the tenor. The song thus presents a series of duets in counterpoint, sung by the woman and the man and the horn and the man. It will be noted that the same rhymes appear in the first and fourth stanzas, the second and fifth stanzas, and the third and sixth stanzas. However, since these pairs of stanzas make up duets, the rhyme words actually come very close together. In the song, 'The May with Blossoms Frail,' the poet imitates the sounds of nature and with a virtuosity unexcelled even in his baroque age. The effect of such onomatopoeia is heightened by a brilliant display of rhyme in which also the emphasis is on sound rather than meaning. In such works as this Wolkenstein almost completely subordinated poetic qualities to musical qualities. The song was inspired and influenced by a three part *virelai* by the French composer Vaillant. The following selection, 'O Margie, Marge, Dear Margaret,' although written when the poet was forty years old, is one of the finest of his love songs. The Margie was Margarete von Schwangau whom he married about the year 1417.

DEPARTED IS MY BOSOM'S WOE

(Zergangen ist meins herzen wê)

Departed is my bosom's woe,
since ice begins to melt and flow
from Seuser hills and down from Flack;
so I heard Mosmair say.
The mists of earth have been released
the springs and streamlets have increased
from Kastelrut to the Isack;
this makes my spirits gay.
The birds within these woods of mine
which lie near Castle Hauenstein
pour forth sweet music from their throats
with happy heart and voice.
From *do* the song goes up to *la*
and down again to trill with *fa*
and sharp and clear are all the notes
so, feathered friends, rejoice.

'What is this gossiper below
who interrupts my singing so?
If it offends him, let him go;
it's all the same to me.'
'Although his voice cause us to fear,
I trust the one who sounds sincere;
it's well that counterfeit this year
can still demand a fee.'

'ATTACK!' SPOKE SIR MICHAEL VON WOLKENSTEIN

('Nû huss!' sprach der Michel von Wolkenstein)

'Attack!' spoke Sir Michael von Wolkenstein;
'Let's get them!' spoke Oswald von Wolkenstein;
'Let fly!' spoke Sir Leonard von Wolkenstein,
'from Greifenstein we'll send them quickly on their way.'

And then a rain of fire began to fall
down on the heads beneath the castle wall
and burned on armor, helmets, bows and all;
they left these as they ran, which caused us no dismay.

Their heavy weapons, tents, and fire shield
were burned to ashes in the upper field;
I hear an evil loan will evil yield
and thus we're glad to give Duke Friedrich all his pay.

O TELL ME, LOVE, WHAT DOES IT MEAN

(Sag an, herzlieb, nû was bedeutet)

'O tell me, love, what does it mean for us,
                    this loud and frightening hail,
these tones that swell?'
'Aa-hoo, get up, your nakedness conceal.'

'My own, why should this stranger come and
                    cause us sadly to lament
your leaving me!'
'Aa-hoo, aa-hoo, soon now the sun will shine.'

'Be on your way,   though you would stay,
hear, hear, this morn   the sounding horn!
Quick, up! Jump up! Hurry up!
The birds are singing in the wood: the blackbird,
                    thrush, the finch,
and a bird that calls itself cuckoo.'

'Now, lady, hear the horn's sad wail;
hill and dale,   every vale   tells its tale,
and I hear the nightingale.
The crimson of the morning rises from the blue;
                                        blow well,
O watchman, your vexation I can feel.

'A wind blows from the orient,
unspent   it lights the firmament
and turns our joy to discontent.
My tender, loving maiden, the horn now thunders
                                        angrily.
I hear you, horn. You grieve this maid of mine.

'Away, away, away, away!
Longing dismay,   murderous day,
our pain cannot withstand you any more.
Goodbye, my dearest love, I'll soon come back to you.'

THE MAY WITH BLOSSOMS FRAIL

(Der mai mit lieber zal)

The May with blossoms frail
has decked the earth to good avail,
mountain, meadow, hill, and dale.
The birds rehearse each scale,
with ringing   and singing   loudly hail
the finch and thrush, the lark and nightingale.
The angry cuckoo sped
with beating wings outspread
after little birds, who fled.
This is what he said:
'Cuckoo, cuckoo, cuckoo,
give me my due,
that will I have from you.
My hunger   makes me younger,
quicker to pursue.'

238

'Beware!   O where
to flee?'   So cried the chickadee.
Goldfinch, titmouse, thrush, now come and sing:
'Oci and too-ee   too-ee   too-ee   too-ee
oci oci oci oci oci oci
fi fideli fideli fideli fi,
ci cieriri ci ci cieriri,
ci ri ciwigg cidiwigg fici fici.'
Thus sang the cuckoo: 'Kawa wa coo coo.'

'Raco,' the raven spoke,
'my voice, too, is sweet,
wheat   I adore,
this song outpour:
"Give more!   Encore!   I implore!"'
'Liri liri liri liri liri liri lon,'
thus sang the lark,   thus sang the lark, thus
                                    sang the lark.
'I sing of a woodthrush,   I sing of a woodthrush,
                        I sing of a woodthrush,'
comes ringing from the forest.
'You court,   disport,
harry,   are merry,
here and there,
just as does our pastor,
cidiwigg cidiwigg cidiwigg,
cificigo cificigo cificigo nightingale,
whose singing rivals the beauty of the grail.'

'Neigh neigh neigh,' cried out the colt,
'let us all sing too!'
'Moo,'   the cows say,
the donkeys bray:
'Put the sack   upon my back!'
'Heehaw heehaw heehaw heehaw heehaw heehaw
                                    come,'
so cried the mule,   so cried the mule, so
                        cried the mule.

'Be silent!' said the miller's wife,
'Get up!' spoke the farmer's wife,
'Move along for all your life,
bray if you will, I say, but walk,
don't balk,   or else the hawk
will tear your hide with many a squawk!
Go on, go on, go on, go on!
Off with your harness!
Get along, Walburg!
Stir yourself as you should,
Weidmann, and run and graze within the wood.'

O MARGIE, MARGE, DEAR MARGARET

(Sim Gredli, Gret, traut Gredelein)

'O Margie, Marge,   dear Margaret,
for whom I yearn   and would caress,
may thy good name   thou ever keep.'
'Whate'er the charge,   Os, my pet,
from thee I'll learn   true faithfulness
and ever aim   thy praise to reap.'
'I greet   these words and shall engrave
them in the bottom of my heart
as from thy rosy lips they part.'
'My sweet,   this too is what I crave,
and I'll never waiver.'
'I'll think of thy favor.'
'Think, dearest Ossie, just of me,
thy Marge will bring delight to thee'.

'Thou canst not give,   nor I desire
more joy than when   thou hast my form
held fast, as one locked in a cell.'
'For thee I'll live   and shall not tire
of holding then;   I'll keep thee warm
with pleasure, and shall do it well.'
'My dear,   I owe thee gratitude

and I shall ne'er forget thy love;
thou'rt always she I'm dreaming of.'
'No fear   that I'll be mean or rude
needst thou have, my treasure.'
'My thanks can have no measure.'
'O, dearest man, I feel so good
when I embrace thee as I would.'

'I cannot know   more joy than this:
thy love and wondrous body, too,
which lustfully to mine is pressed.'
'I overflow   with keenest bliss
and thrill with passion through and through
whene'er thy hands caress my breast.'
'My bride,   the best of sugarbread,
whose sweetness flows through all thy limbs,
is that thy lovelight never dims.'
'Abide,   and trust what I have said,
Os, with faith unbending.'
'Be thy love unending!'
'Let fortune never separate
us two, nor harm a love so great!'

The last of Wolkenstein's songs to be given here is a translation, not of the work as he composed it, but as it appeared in the *Rostocker Liederbuch* twenty years after his death. A comparison of the form of the popular version with that of the original clearly illustrates some of the changes which take place during the transition from a sophisticated minnesong to a folksong. The original stanza had four long lines with caesuras and two half lines. The rhyme scheme was as follows, with rhymes *a*, *b*, *c*, and *f* being repeated in each stanza:

a	b
c	
d	e
d	e
d	e
f	

It will be noted that the version below has lost (or nearly so) the caesuras, greatly simplified the rhyme pattern, and reduced the inter-stanza rhyme to that of the last line—also that there is no longer complete consistency from stanza to stanza with regard to rhyme scheme. However, the 'folksong' is as pleasing as the original, perhaps more so.

AWAKE, MY LOVE, FOR IN THE EAST

(Wach uff, myn hort, er lucht dort her)

'Awake, my love, for in the east
the rising sun sends forth its rays
and presses through the twilight haze.
How clear and blue is heaven's light
as morning comes in armor bright.
I fear the day is breaking.'

'Alas, with sorrow I must flee.
I hear the birds in bush and tree
the morn with joyous voices hail
and hear again the nightingale.
My bitter fate must still prevail,
although my heart is aching.

'Farewell, thou treasure of my heart,
I grieve that we at last must part.'
To leave her thus is sore dismay,
her red lips cause me still to stay
when bitter death drives me away,
my fear and sadness waking.

INDEX OF FIRST LINES

Middle High German texts of the poems as well as the location of the original manuscripts can be found in the following anthologies. For many of the songs several manuscript versions are extant and, in some cases, that used here differs slightly from the text indicated.

BSM: Bartsch, Karl. *Die Schweizer Minnesänger.* Darmstadt, 1964.

BM de Boor, Helmut. *Mittelalter.* Munich, 1965.

DTO: *Denkmäler der Tonkunst in Österreich.* XVIII (1959) and XLI (1960).

HM: Hagen, Friedrich von der. *Minnesinger.* 5 vols. Leipzig, 1838-1861.

KMF: Kraus, Carl von. *Des Minnesangs Frühling.* Stuttgart, 1962.

KDL: Kraus, Carl von. *Deutsche Liederdichter des 13. Jahrhunderts.* 2 vols. Tübingen, 1952.

KWV: Kraus, Carl von. *Die Gedichte Walthers von der Vogelweide.* Berlin, 1962.

LUL: Lachmann, Karl. *Ulrich von Lichtenstein.* Berlin, 1841.

LOM: Lang, Margarete. *Ostdeutscher Minnesang.* Lindau, 1958.

LDDM: Leyen, Friedrich von der. *Deutsche Dichtung des Mittelalters.* Frankfurt, 1962.

MAM: Moret, André. *Anthologie du Minnesang.* Paris, 1949.

MSAP: Münzer, G. *Das Singebuch des Adam Puschman nebst den Originalmelodien.* Leipzig, 1906.

PFM: Pfaff, Fridrich. *Der Minnesang des 12. bis 14. Jahrhunderts.* Stuttgart, ca. 1890.

RLHM: Runge, Paul. *Die Lieder des Hugo von Montfort.* Leipzig, 1906.

SSM: Seagrave, Barbara and Thomas, Wesley. *The Songs of the Minnesingers.* Urbana, 1966.

WDLM: Wehrli, Max. *Deutsche Lyrik des Mittelalters.* Zürich, 1962.

WLN: Wiessner, Edmund. *Die Lieder Neidharts.* Tübingen, 1955.

ich partere dich durch mine vrowen (HM IV, 810), 168
ich sach boten des sumeres daz waren bluomen also rot (KMF 9), 54
ich sach drey starker warn fast gross (LDDM 84), 23
ich saz uf eime steine (KWV 9), 119
ich sihe wol daz got wunder kan (PFM 19), 70
ich wache umb eines ritters lip (KDL I, 177), 148
ich was ein chint so wolgetan (BM 1740), 42
ich will zu land aussreiten sprach sich maister hiltebrant (LDDM
    18), 31
ich wil truren varen lan (LDDM 237), 39
ich zoch mir einen valken mere danne ein jar (KMF 5), 52
in dem luftesüezen meien (KDL I, 459), 156
ine gesach die heide (WLN 29), 129
in gotes namen fara wir (WDLM 478), 13
in so hoher swebender wunne (PFM 53), 86
in weiz wiech singe (KDL I, 429), 154
ir sult sprechen willekomen (KWV 79), 116
ist iht mere schoenes (KDL I, 514), 190
jamer ist mir entsprungen (HM IV, 774), 98
jo stuont ich nechtint spate vor dinem bette (KMF 5), 52
ju in erde (BM 406), 4
junger man von tzwenzich iaren (HM IV, 794), 197
kint bereitet iuch der sliten uf daz is (WLN 56), 136
klageliche not (BSM 110), 160
lanc bin ich geweset verdaht (KMF 194), 87
leit machet sorge vil liebe wunne (KMF 4), 51
lieber bote nu wirp also (KMF 240), 105
manger wunne bilde (MAM 246), 211
meyie scone kum io tzuo (HM IV, 815), 170
mich dunket niht so guotes noch so lobesam (KMF 1), 61
mich straft ain wachter des morgens frü (RLHM 29), 225
min frowe diu wil lonen mir (PFM 185), 177
minne gebiutet mir daz ich singe (BSM 2), 77
mir erwelten miniu ougen einen kindeschen man (KMF 9), 53
mir hat her gerhart atze ein pfert (KWV 143), 121
mir ist als ich niht lebende si swenn ich entnücke sere (BM 546),
    211
mir ist daz herze wunt (KMF 46), 69

mit saelden müeze ich hiute ufstan (KWV 31), 124
mit sange wande ich mine sorge krenken (BSM 4), 78
myn trurichlichez klagen (KDL I, 15), 204
myn vroud ist gar czugangyn nu horit iamirliche clag (DTO XLI, 67), 218
nahtegal sing einen don mit sinne (WDLM 276), 41
nie man tzu vro sol prysen (HM IV, 790), 208
niemen ist ein saelic man (PFM 78), 90
niemen seneder suoche an mich deheinen rat (BM 1521), 102
nu alrest leb ich mir werde (KWV 18), 122
nu biten wir den heiligen geist (WDLM 476), 14
nu huss sprach der michel von wolkenstein (DTO XVIII, 47), 237
nun will ich aber heben an (LDDM 679), 33
o du brennender berg o du userwelte sunne (WDLM 482), 17
owe daz nach liebe gat (KDL I, 13), 203
owe miner gar virlornen jare (BM 1752), 14
owe sol aber iemer me (BM 1671), 83
sach ieman die vrowen (PFM 54), 84
sag an herzlieb nu was bedeutet (DTO XVIII, 17), 237
sag an wachter wie was es tag (RLHM 34), 226
salve regina mater misercordie (SSM 124), 182
seneder friundinne bote nu sage dem schonen wibe (KMF 31), 57
sie darf mich des zihen niet (KMF 58), 66
sie jehent der sumer der si hie (LDDM 261), 103
sie wanent dem tode entrunnen sin (PFM 24), 70
si is so gut ende ouch so scone (KMF 78), 74
sim gredli gret traut gredelein (DTO XVIII, 46), 240
sinc an guldin huon ich gibe dir weize (WLN 58), 139
sine klawen (KDL I, 597), 94
sit die sonne her liehten skin (PFM 29), 74
sit si mir niht lonen wil (BSM 170), 193
siu ist mir liep und liebet mir für alliu wip (KDL I, 276), 163
si wunderwol gemachet wip (KWV 74), 112
slafestu vriedel ziere (KMF 39), 58
so die bluomen uz dem grase dringent (KWV 63), 115
sol ich nu klagen die heide wa ist ein jamer groz (KDL I, 230), 161
so we den merkaeren die habent min übele gedaht (KMF 8), 53
so wol dir sumerwunne (KMF 33), 56

so wol dir wip wie reine ein nam (LDDM 269), 103
sta bi la mich den wint an waejen (KDL I, 21), 146
stetit puella bi einem boume (BM 1668), 40
swa eyn vriunt dem andern vriunde bigestat (KMF 20), 30
swaz hie gat umbe (WDLM 7), 40
swelch mensche wird ze einer stunt (WDLM 484), 18
swelch vrowe sendet lieben man (PFM 78), 92
swen gerende liute gerne suochent (HM III, 46), 197
swenn die tid also gestat (PFM 34), 73
swenne ich schine so muost du lühten (WDLM 480), 17
swenne ich stan al eine in minem hemede (KMF 5), 51
tief furt truobe (LDDM 219), 28
ubermuot diu alte (LDDM 219), 29
uf dem berge und in dem tal (WLN 16), 134
uf der linden obene da sanc ein kleinez vogellin (KMF 32), 60
under der linden (KWV 52), 111
uns hat der winter geschat über al (KWV 52), 109
ursprinc bluomen loup uz dringen (KDL I, 600), 97
vil lieber vriund vremden daz ist schedelich (KMF 4), 51
vil suze senfte toterinne (PFM 62), 85
vil wol gelobter got wie selten ich dich prise (KWV 33), 124
wach uff myn hort er lucht dort her (LOM 70), 242
waer diu werlt alliu min (KMF 1), 41
waz ist daz liehte daz luzet her vür (BSM 258), 188
weistu wie der igel sprach (KMF 23), 30
weka wekh die zarten lieben (RLHM 52), 227
welchs ist ein wald on laub (LDDM 83), 23
wene herze wenent ougen (WDLM 496), 19
were alle die welt min (WDLM 484), 18
wer gab dir minne den gewalt (KWV 78), 115
wes mansdu mich leides min vil liebe liep (KMF 4), 51
wibes güete niemen mac (KDL I, 428), 153
wil iemen nach eren die zit wol vertriben (KDL I, 444), 155
willekomme varender man (LDDM 84), 24
winter diniu meil (WLN 120), 141
wip vil schone nu far du sam mir (PFM 6), 50
wir suln den kochen raten (KWV 21), 120
wir sun den winder in stuben enpfahen (KDL I, 33), 185

wol dan her meyie ich ghebe uch des de hulde (HM IV, 815), 172
zart libste frau in liber acht (SSM 190), 231
ze fröiden nahet alle tage (PFM 73), 105
zergangen ist meins herzen we (DTO XVIII, 50), 236

INDEX OF AUTHORS

The page number given refers to the beginning of the main body of discussion concerning the author.

UNIVERSITY OF NORTH CAROLINA
STUDIES IN THE GERMANIC LANGUAGES
AND LITERATURES